ROCKY MOUNTAIN TRAIN ROBBERIES

True Stories of Notorious Bandits and Infamous Escapades

W. C. JAMESON

TWODOT®

Guilford, Connecticut
Helena, Montana

A · TWODOT® · BOOK

An imprint and registered trademark of The Rowman & Littlefield Publishing Group, Inc.
4501 Forbes Blvd., Ste. 200
Lanham, MD 20706
www.rowman.com

Distributed by NATIONAL BOOK NETWORK

British Library Cataloguing in Publication Information available

Library of Congress Cataloging-in-Publication Data

Names: Jameson, W. C., 1942- author.
Title: Rocky Mountain train robberies / W. C. Jameson.
Description: Guilford, Connecticut : TwoDot, [2019] | Includes
    bibliographical references and index. |
Identifiers: LCCN 2018027398 (print) | LCCN 2018042476 (ebook) | ISBN
    9781493033379 (e-book) | ISBN 9781493033362 (pbk. : alk. paper) | ISBN
    9781493033379 (ebook)
Subjects: LCSH: Pacific and Mountain States—History. | Train robberies—
    Pacific and Mountain States—History. | Brigands and robbers—
    Pacific and Mountain States—History.
Classification: LCC F718 (ebook) | LCC F718 .J36 2019 (print) | DDC 978—
dc23 LC record available at https://lccn.loc.gov/2018027398

♾™ The paper used in this publication meets the minimum requirements of American National Standard for Information Sciences—Permanence of Paper for Printed Library Materials, ANSI/NISO Z39.48-1992.

Printed in the United States of America

CONTENTS

IDAHO

MONTANA

NEVADA

NEW MEXICO

WYOMING

INTRODUCTION

For most people, the subject of train robberies calls to mind the dramatic exploits of outlaws such as Butch Cassidy and the Sundance Kid, Harvey "Kid Curry" Logan, the Dalton Gang, the Doolin Gang, and Frank and Jesse James, to name a few. As a result of their colorful lives, their derring-do, and their flaunting of laws and institutions, these outlaws and others like them have left an indelible impression on the imaginations of most Americans. Ask people to name the US presidents of the nineteenth century, and most cannot come up with more than one or two, if that. But ask them to name noted outlaws of the same period, and they can recall the James Gang, Cassidy, and more, with ease.

This instant recognition of outlaws is likely based on the abundance of information and material on such men in the form of historical and biographic publications, novels, films, and television documentaries. Unfortunately, most people "know" these interesting and distinctive outlaws from the treatment they've received in film and television. In truth, their lives were far different from what has been portrayed and oftentimes considerably more adventurous and dangerous than we have come to believe.

Between 1870 and 1937, the Rocky Mountain West served as the setting for some of the best-known train robberies in the history of the United States. This region includes Arizona, Colorado, Idaho, Montana, New Mexico, Nevada, and Wyoming. The train robberies that took place in this vast territory propelled to the forefront of American outlaw personalities the likes of Butch Cassidy, Harry "The Sundance Kid" Longabaugh, Harvey "Kid Curry" Logan, Thomas "Black Jack" Ketchum, William "Black Jack" Christian, Burt Alvord, and more. Likewise, it introduced the American public to famous lawmen such as Buckey O'Neill, Tom Horn, Jeff Milton, John Fly, and others.

The following pages contain accounts of thirty-seven train robberies perpetrated in seven states found in America's Rocky Mountain West. The states are arranged alphabetically, and the robberies in each are ordered chronologically. A glossary of pertinent railroad terms is included at the end of the book.

ARIZONA

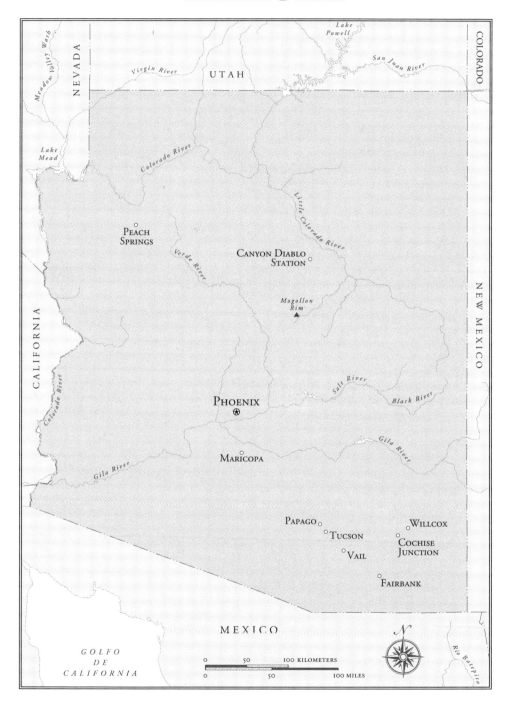

CHAPTER 1

PAPAGO, APRIL 27, 1887

It was 9:30 p.m. on the night of April 27, 1887, and Southern Pacific engineer Colonel Bill Harper anticipated arriving at the Tucson station within the hour. The westbound run had gone smoothly and uneventfully, and Harper was looking forward to some time off. A short distance ahead was the tiny settlement of Papago. Just before reaching it, Harper spotted a red lantern swinging back and forth ahead on the track, a warning for the train to stop. Such a signal was often employed in emergency situations like rockslides, washouts, and loose rails, all of which resulted in delays. As Harper slowed the train, he spotted a number of obstructions on the rails ahead that appeared intended to derail the train if it did not stop.

As soon as the train was pulled to a halt, a man carrying two revolvers appeared out of the dark and fired shots at the express car. A moment later, the stranger climbed aboard the locomotive, pointed one of his weapons at Harper, and ordered him to climb down. The robber then marched the engineer down the tracks to the express car. When they arrived, at least four other outlaws were already there attempting to pry open the car door. All of the men wore black masks.

Inside the express car, Wells, Fargo and Company messenger Charles F. Smith, alerted to a potential robbery by the gunfire, gathered up several canvas bags containing a total of $3,500 in gold and stuffed them into the express car's stove. All the while, the outlaws outside the car were yelling for the messenger to open the door.

Failing to pry open the express car door or to convince messenger Smith to open it, the robbers attached a charge of black powder to it and compelled Harper to light the fuse. Harper told the outlaws that such a measure was not necessary, that he could talk the messenger into opening the door. Smith finally relented and slid the door open to allow the outlaws inside. With this accomplished, the robbers uncoupled the express car and the baggage car from the rest of the train. Following this, they removed the debris from the track and ordered engineer Harper to climb back into the locomotive cab and pull ahead two lengths. Harper had no sooner repositioned the train than two of the bandits climbed into the cab and threw him out. Manipulating the controls, they ran the locomotive six miles down the tracks toward Tucson. Later, engineer Harper told railroad investigators that he was convinced the robbers were experienced railroaders as they were quite familiar with operating the locomotive. As the train sped westward, the remaining robbers went through the packages in the express car searching for money and gold.

The bandits found only two packages of money. One contained $1,200, the other $500. They also took two packages of postage stamps. As the robbery was taking place, a brakeman who had earlier slipped away made his way a short distance up the track to Pantano Station, where he had a telegram sent to law enforcement authorities. Pima County sheriff Charles A. Shibell quickly formed a posse and enlisted Indian trackers. The posse was joined by a troop of cavalry.

Wells, Fargo lost no time in offering a reward of $1,000 for the capture of each of the robbers. Word soon spread throughout the region that the bandits were members of the notorious Doc Smart Gang. Several men were immediately arrested at various locations in the county, but each provided alibis. Wells, Fargo officials reported that $5,000 had been taken and they were prepared to file an insurance claim on that amount. It was later adjusted to $3,227.60.

The posses had no luck in picking up the tracks of the train robbers, and after several weeks of a dead-end investigation, the robbery of the Southern Pacific train at Papago became little more than a memory. And then, on August 10, less than four months later, robbers struck again.

CHAPTER 2

VAIL, AUGUST 10, 1887

Three and a half months after the April robbery of the westbound Southern Pacific at Papago, Arizona, the same train was robbed again at Vail, not far from the site of the first robbery. The engineer spotted a waving lantern ahead and began applying the brakes. This time, however, he did not react in time, and the train surged onto the obstacles placed on the track and overturned. Engineer Jim Guthrie and fireman R. T. Bradford were injured. The robbers fired their weapons at the two railroad men, one of the bullets neatly clipping off a portion of Bradford's mustache.

Wells, Fargo messenger Charles F. Smith was again on duty in the express car and heard the robbers approaching. When they arrived, they called out to him and told him that his trick of stuffing the gold shipment in the stove would not work this time. It was clear to Smith that the same men involved in the previous robbery—the Doc Smart Gang were attempting this one. In any case, Smith refused to open the door.

The bandits wasted no time negotiating with Smith. They applied a charge of black powder to the door and blew a hole in it. They forced the mail clerk to crawl through it and instructed him to convince Smith that he needed to stop resisting. Smith agreed and opened the door to the bandits. Moving quickly, the robbers worked their way through the express car, opening bags and taking whatever they deemed valuable. Minutes later, they jumped from the car, ran to their horses, and raced away eastward toward the Rincon Mountains. The *Arizona Daily Star* reported that the outlaws got away with $70,000, but knowledgeable sources claimed that only $1,000 to $2,000 was taken.

Once again, posses were formed, Indian trackers were recruited, and a troop of cavalry volunteered for the search. Even noted lawman Virgil Earp volunteered his services. The tracks of the train robbers were found and followed, the trail eventually leading to a cave at a location known as Mountain Springs, twelve miles from the site of the robbery. During the pursuit, a heavy rainstorm forced the lawmen and the military to abandon the chase.

Some confusion exists about who actually belonged to the Doc Smart Gang. While known gang members included Doc Smart, John Myers (or Meyers), W. T. Skidmore, Jake Smith, A. W. Snyder, and George Willis, five additional men were arrested for the robbery several days later: Si Blunt, T. Joseph Brooks, T. J. Hart, James Johnson, and Larry Sheehan. Johnson and Sheehan, it was learned, were aliases for two brothers, Jim and John Cravens. The Cravens brothers were wanted for rustling livestock in Williamson County, Texas. All these men were believed to be members of the Doc Smart Gang, but Smart was not among them. The outlaws were tried, but only the Cravens brothers were found guilty. They were sent to the Yuma Territorial Prison.

Two months later another Southern Pacific train was stopped near El Paso, Texas. Leading the gang of robbers was Doc Smart. Wasting little time, Smart and several members of his gang made their way to the express car, where they found messenger Charles F. Smith on duty once again. Unbeknownst to the robbers, messenger Smith had grown weary of being held up. This time he slid the door open, produced two revolvers, and as the robbers approached his car, opened fire, killing two of them: Jake Smith and John Myers. Routed in this manner, the remainder of the outlaws ran for their horses and rode away.

Days later, railroad detectives tracked the rest of bandits to a boarding house in El Paso, where they were arrested. Among them was Doc Smart. After being found guilty of involvement in three train robberies, Smart was sentenced to life in prison. While serving his sentence, Smart decided to commit suicide. He somehow obtained a revolver and fired three shots into his head. Bizarrely, none of the bullets penetrated his skull. Years later, President Benjamin Harrison pardoned Doc Smart.

CHAPTER 3

CANYON DIABLO STATION, MARCH 1, 1889

Canyon Diablo is located thirty miles east of Flagstaff, Arizona, and a few miles north of the tiny Interstate 40 community of Two Guns. In 1881, the Atlantic and Pacific Railroad, in its westward push, encountered a 255-foot-deep, 540-foot-wide canyon at the site. A railroad bridge spanning the canyon was completed in 1882, and a train station was established nearby. A new bridge was constructed in 1947, and trains continue to cross as they head east and west. At one time the population of Canyon Diablo was estimated to be two thousand. The train station has been long abandoned, and today Canyon Diablo, Spanish for "devil's canyon," is a ghost town.

By 1889, Canyon Diablo had lost most of its population and consisted of little more than a few occupied dwellings, some corrals and loading pens, a trading post, and the Atlantic and Pacific train station. During its heyday, Canyon Diablo had seen gambling, prostitution, and gunfights. Local sheriffs didn't last long in the job, and those who were not gunned down soon sought other lines of work. With all the hell-raising and violence associated with the town, there had never been a train robbery—that is, not until March 1, 1889.

In 1889 there was little to do in Canyon Diablo. Likely in search of some adventure, four out-of-work cowhands—Long John Halford, Daniel Harvick, John Smith, and William D. Starin (also

11

spelled Sterin)—decided to rob a train. As far as can be determined, there was no planning involved, and the robbery was a spontaneous act. As the eastbound Atlantic and Pacific No. 2 train took on water and wood at the station, the four cowhands approached. One came upon the fireman, who was examining the underside of the locomotive's boiler. Pulling a gun, he forced the fireman, along with the engineer, to lead the outlaws to the express car.

On arriving at the express car, they found the door slid back and the messenger standing in the opening. As the robbers, fireman, and engineer approached, the messenger greeted them good-naturedly and asked how they were doing. John Smith, suspecting that another messenger, perhaps armed, was stationed just inside the car, feared an ambush. On examining the interior, however, Smith found the car unoccupied.

Bolted to the floor of the express car was a large metal safe. As the outlaws examined it, the conductor arrived outside the car, followed by several passengers who were curious as to what was transpiring. One of the robbers fired his revolver into the air, sending the newcomers scrambling back to the coaches.

The messenger, still in a seemingly good mood, informed the robbers that as the large safe, called a through safe, was on a time lock, he was unable to open it. One of the robbers noticed a smaller safe nearby and at gunpoint ordered the messenger to open it, which he did. The contents of the safe were scooped up and stuffed into three canvas sacks found nearby. Bidding the messenger, fireman, and engineer good-bye, the robbers exited the express car, walked over to where they had tied their horses, secured the bags to their saddles, and rode away toward the south.

After traveling five miles, the robbers pulled into a grove of trees to rest their horses. Finding a stream nearby, as well as abundant firewood, they decided to make camp for the night. Later that evening, as their meal cooked, the four men emptied the robbery loot from the bags and divided it among themselves. According to robber Daniel Harvick during an interview years later, the take amounted to $7,000 in cash along with some jewelry. A few days after the robbery, the express company reported a loss of $40,000 and filed an insurance claim for that amount. (Train robbery history is replete with examples of supposedly reputable express companies inflating losses.) Before turning in for the night, the gang buried the jewelry, along with their rifles, at this campsite.

The next morning after breakfast, the four train robbers decided it would be best to separate and reunite later. Harvick and Starin rode southeast toward the Black Falls of the Little Colorado River. Halford and Smith traveled north into the Navajo reservation.

As soon as it could be managed, Yavapai County sheriff William O. "Buckey" O'Neill was notified of the robbery. (As a result of county realignment, Canyon Diablo is located in Coconino County today.) O'Neill summoned two of his deputies, Jim Black and Ed St. Clair, along with two railroad detectives, Fred Fornoff and Carl Holton. In a short time, O'Neill and his posse picked up the trail of Halford and Smith on the Navajo reservation. Spurring their mounts to greater speed, the lawmen closed the distance between themselves and the outlaws each day. Two weeks later, the tracks led them into Utah, where the lawmen began encountering the outlaws' campfires, which were still warm.

O'Neill shortly noted that the tracks of the two robbers had become four. O'Neill assumed the remaining two bandits had rejoined their comrades. The next day, the lawmen caught up with the train robbers near Wah Weep Canyon on the Arizona-Utah border. On spotting the oncoming lawmen, the outlaws opened fire. During the initial fusillade, O'Neill's horse was killed. O'Neill got pinned beneath the animal as it fell to the ground. With assistance from railroad detective Holton, the sheriff was extricated. Undeterred, O'Neill continued charging into the outlaws' campsite, and moments later all four were arrested.

Returning the four train robbers to Yavapai County turned out to be nearly as much an adventure as pursuing them. Not wanting to make the long ride back through extremely rough country

Captain Buckey O'Neill

to Canyon Diablo, O'Neill, with his prisoners in tow, traveled instead to Salt Lake City. There, he purchased nine train tickets for Denver—one each for himself, his deputies, the railroad detectives, and the four prisoners. At Denver, he purchased nine more tickets for Prescott, Arizona. During the return trip, one of the prisoners escaped and was recaptured later.

All in all, O'Neill spent just over $8,000 during his pursuit and capture of the Atlantic and Pacific train robbers. He received newspaper headlines filled with praise for his efforts and was recognized by Arizona Territory governor Louis Wolley. Despite the successful capture and positive response, O'Neill's request for reimbursement for the full amount his expenses was rejected. Yavapai County officials approved an amount of $5,800. O'Neill sued and lost on appeal.

Robbers Halford, Harvick, Smith, and Starin were tried, found guilty of train robbery, and sentenced to the Yuma Territorial Prison. All four were pardoned eight years later. Using an alias, Starin joined Theodore Roosevelt's Rough Riders. He was killed in action on July 1, 1898, during the Battle of San Juan Hill in Cuba. Ironically, Buckey O'Neill also enlisted in the Rough Riders and perished in action on the same day.

CHAPTER 4

MARICOPA, OCTOBER 1, 1894

The holdup of the Southern Pacific train at Maricopa is noteworthy because, in the words of author Richard Patterson, it "has been described as one of the most amateurish assaults in the annals of train robbery."

Maricopa is located in the Gila River valley forty miles south of downtown Phoenix. Because of the abundant wells, as well as nearby freshwater rivers and streams, the area became an important stop for travelers. Here, a relay station was constructed for the San Antonio–San Diego Mail Line, a stagecoach service. Later, the Butterfield Overland Mail took over the company. Today, Maricopa boasts a population of forty-eight thousand.

As the midnight hour approached on October 1, 1894 (one account gives the date as September 30), the eastbound Southern Pacific No. 19 train had finished loading freight and boarding passengers and was preparing to pull away from the station. Moments later, as the train got underway, two men who had been perched on the water tank leapt onto the baggage car. This was an unusual tactic. Most train robbers crept up to the train they intended to rob from a place of hiding near the tracks in order to keep from being spotted.

Gerald Cerrin was working as the chief brakeman on the Southern Pacific run this night. He watched as the two would-be robbers landed on the baggage car and made their way to the blind. Cerrin presumed the two men were hobos, so he approached to order them off the train. As he neared the two, he saw that they were wearing masks and carrying revolvers. It was too late; Cerrin was taken captive.

Twenty minutes later, Jim Holliday, the engineer, spotted a waving lantern a short distance ahead on the track—normally a warning of danger. Believing there was a problem, Holliday applied the brakes, and the train slowed. Just before the Southern Pacific came to a halt, one of the bandits who had made his way from the baggage car to the coal tender dropped into the cab of the locomotive, pointed his revolvers at the engineer and fireman, and demanded that they stop the train.

As the train ground to a standstill, a third masked robber approached the engine from a hiding place near the tracks. When he arrived, he ordered Holliday to uncouple the engine from the trailing train. This was an odd command: in a number of successful train robberies, the perpetrators had the uncoupling done behind the express car, separating it from the passenger coaches and preventing potential intrusion by passengers and members of the train crew; the locomotive, pulling the tender and the express car, was then moved some distance down the track, where the robbery could take place uninterrupted. In this case, however, the engineer was ordered to pull the locomotive ahead about one hundred yards, leaving the entire train behind.

As the locomotive moved down the track, the robbers fired shots at the coaches, presumably to keep the crew and passengers ducking for cover and less likely to interfere. By the time the three robbers arrived at the express car, the messenger, George Mitchell, had decided to offer no resistance and opened the door to admit them. Since messengers were responsible for the cargo carried in the express car, and because they often lost their jobs if they clearly had not done everything in their power to thwart a robbery, this was an unusual move. Mitchell, after hearing the gunfire, likely determined that opening the door would be easier than resisting. Occasionally when a messenger refused to open the door, bandits applied dynamite, with the resulting explosion oftentimes damaging the express car and injuring its occupant.

After stopping the locomotive for the second time, the engineer and fireman walked back to the rest of the train to witness the goings-on. Messenger Mitchell may have felt somewhat secure in the notion that the safe had recently been equipped with brand-new locks and could only be opened by express agents at certain stations along the route. When the robbers saw that they would not be able to get into the large safe, they settled on the cash from the local safe, a total of only $160. Unhappy with this small sum, one of the robbers suggested they invade the coaches and rob the passengers. They turned to their captive, brakeman Cerrin, and inquired about the passengers on this run. Cerrin, a veteran trainman, had envisioned this possibility. He told the robbers that the passengers were by and large a poor lot with little in the way of possessions or money. The robbers bought Cerrin's lie. As they were about to climb out of the express car, they took messenger Mitchell's pocket watch.

After racing for their horses, which were tied to some trees a short distance away, the robbers mounted up and left the scene. As they disappeared into the night, the engineer and fireman undertook the short hike back to the locomotive. They backed it up to the train, recoupled the tender, and returned to the Maricopa station. The engineer alerted the station manager, and telegrams were sent to local law enforcement officials, Wells, Fargo & Company, and Southern Pacific.

As they fled the scene of the robbery, the perpetrators left an abundance of tracks. A sheriff from a nearby town spotted three sets of hoofprints heading away from the point where the engineer said the bandits had tied their mounts. The tracks led to a location west of Phoenix. There, the sheriff and his posse came upon a newly made camp. Three horses that appeared to have been ridden hard and long were tied nearby, but no one was about. Rifles and shotguns were still in the saddle scabbards. The sheriff, whose name was Murphy, determined that the outlaws had walked over to a nearby pasture in search of forage for the horses. The lawmen took up positions in hiding and waited for the robbers to return.

A half hour later, a man walked into the campsite carrying a load of hay in his arms. He was surprised by a command to drop the hay and raise his hands. Reacting badly, he reached for his revolver. Before he could pull his weapon from the holster, he was dropped by a load of buckshot fired by one of the posse members. Not far away, the other two robbers, likewise returning to the camp with hay, dropped their loads and fled on foot in the opposite direction.

After seeing to the wounded outlaw, the sheriff learned that he was Frank Armer, a local ranch hand. The watch taken from messenger Mitchell was found in one of his pockets, and Armer was arrested. It emerged that Armer hung out with a man named Oscar Armstrong, a ne'er-do-well wanted for robbing a café at Fort Wingate, New Mexico. (At least one account offers the surname Rogers for Armer's companion.) Presumed to be one of Armer's accomplices in the Southern Pacific holdup, Armstrong was arrested several weeks later near Tacna Station, forty miles east of Yuma.

The third robber, believed by authorities to be John Donovan, who went by the aliases Bryant and O'Bryan, had recently been released from prison. He was never captured.

Armer and Armstrong were both tried for train robbery, found guilty, and sentenced to hang. During this time, train robbery was a capital offense in Arizona. Both sentences were later commuted to forty years, and the men were sent to the Yuma Territorial Prison. (One account states that the sentence was for thirty years.) During his incarceration, Armer made at least three attempts to escape.

While in prison, Armer contracted tuberculosis. So weakened and pitiful was the former train robber that officials chose to release him. He was sent to the home of his mother, where he died a short time later.

Armstrong (or Rogers) served eleven years of his forty-year sentence and was released for "exemplary conduct."

CHAPTER 5

WILLCOX, JANUARY 30, 1895

In 1895, Willcox lay in a relatively remote and sparsely settled part of Cochise County in southeastern Arizona, seventy-five miles due east of Tucson. Originally founded in 1880 and named Maley, the town was renamed in 1889 for Orlando B. Willcox, at the time a somewhat prominent cattleman in that part of the territory. The population of Willcox in 1895 was around four hundred, counting all those living on ranches in the surrounding area. Today the population is just under four thousand.

One of the first buildings erected in Willcox was a station for the Southern Pacific Railroad. On January 30, 1895, the westbound Southern Pacific train made a brief stop at the Willcox station to unload mail. Moments later, as it was pulling away, two men dashed out from hiding and leapt aboard one of the blinds. From there, they made their way to the top of the car and scrambled forward along the others until reaching the tender. After observing the engineer and the fireman for several minutes, the intruders, with revolvers drawn, dropped down into the locomotive cab and ordered the engineer to stop the train, which by this time was two miles out of Willcox.

Once the train had ground to a halt, one of the gunmen ordered the engineer and fireman out of the cab and back down the tracks to the express car. Here, the two railroad men were instructed to uncouple the express and baggage cars from the rest of the train, which consisted of only two coaches and the caboose. This done, the engineer was told to pull the train forward another two miles.

Given the train's odd stopping and proceeding, the Wells, Fargo express car messenger deduced that a robbery was in progress. Hurriedly, he placed anything he deemed important and/or valuable into the safe and locked it. He then slid open the car door and, as the train was making its way down the track, leaped to the ground and hid in the nearby brush for a few moments. When he determined that it was safe to do so, he made his way back to the passenger coaches and recruited two men to walk back to Willcox and notify the sheriff.

When the train was again stopped at the designated location— a remote stretch of open land called Dry Lake—two additional robbers were seen waiting near the tracks. They were mounted and holding the reins of two extra horses.

After entering the express car, the bandits applied a small bundle of dynamite to the express company safe. Among other shipments, the safe contained seven hundred Mexican silver pesos. Following the detonation, they inspected the safe and discovered the charge had had no effect at all. They applied a second with the same result. In the end, it took six charges to blow the safe open, testimony to the perceived inexperience of the robbers. Unfortunately, the sixth blast, the largest of them all, blew up the express car as well as the safe and scattered the contents for several yards in all directions.

The robbers scurried around and gathered up as much of the money as they could find, remounted their horses, and rode away. When he was certain the bandits were gone, the engineer backed the train up to the passenger coaches, recoupled the cars, and returned to Willcox. The train robbers had escaped with approximately $10,000 worth of money. Somehow, they missed most of the Mexican coins later harvested by Wells, Fargo officials who arrived at the scene. Wells, Fargo offered a substantial reward for the train robbers.

Alerted to the robbery, Cochise County sheriff John Fly organized a posse of five men and set out to track the robbers. They followed the trail for several miles but lost it when the robbers rode across a stretch of rocky ground. On returning to Willcox, Fly learned that a man named Grant Wheeler, a known outlaw, had purchased eleven pounds of dynamite, fifty feet of fuse, and several ignition caps at a Willcox hardware store a day or two prior to the robbery. Wheeler was in the company of another man.

The next morning, a man named Moore, who had a ranch four miles out of Willcox, rode into town to inform Sheriff Fly that Grant Wheeler and Joe George had stopped at his house around midnight and requested a meal. Moore noted that the two riders appeared nervous but thought little of it until morning, after they had ridden away and one of Moore's ranch hands related the news of the train robbery.

Later that same day, another nearby cattleman named Yates arrived in town to report that Wheeler and George had ridden onto his ranch wanting to purchase a horse. It was apparent to Yates that Wheeler's horse was crippled and unable to travel much farther. When Yates informed Wheeler that he had no horses to sell, the robber pulled a handgun and stole one of his mounts. Yates told Fly that the two outlaws rode away on the trail that led to Rucker Canyon in the Chiricahua Mountains to the southeast. At the time, Rucker Canyon was a popular hideout for outlaws. Lawmen, Fly among them, feared entering the region. Active pursuit of the Southern Pacific train robbers was halted.

A few weeks passed, and Sheriff Fly received word that Joe George had been killed in Mexico. George was described as being in his late forties or early fifties and rarely getting along with anyone. In Sonora, Mexico, George got into an argument with a Mexican cowhand, who shot and killed him. George had eighteen dollars in his pockets.

Grant Wheeler had come from a respected Mormon family in Utah. He was described as being in his twenties, good-looking, and athletic. In fleeing the law, Wheeler traveled to the ranch of a brother located near Utah's Uintah Mountains. While Sheriff Fly was reluctant to ride into the outlaw lair in Rucker Canyon, he had no qualms about traveling to Utah. Fly had contacts around the area up to and including Utah. From one of them he learned that young Wheeler had landed at the brother's ranch. He also learned that some lawmen and a handful of bounty hunters, all anxious to collect the reward offered by Wells, Fargo, were out to get him. Wheeler learned this as well. As a result, he made plans to leave his brother's ranch and head north to where he was unknown.

He waited too long. As Wheeler was tying his pack to his saddle horse, a posse rode onto the ranch. Seeing that there was no chance of escape, Wheeler pulled his revolver and shot himself in the head. He died instantly. A search of his pockets yielded only a few pennies.

The two outlaws who were waiting for Wheeler and George at Dry Lake were never identified. Some reports of the robbery suggest that only Wheeler and George were involved.

Contrary to the official reports of the Willcox train robbery, stories circulated that the bandits made off with as much as $84,000, some of it in cash and some in gold. If so, we are left wondering what happened to that loot. Speculation is that the outlaws cached it somewhere with the intention of retrieving it when pursuit lessened.

The answer may lie in a discovery made during the early 1900s. Two prospectors were examining outcrops near the Dos Cabezas Mountains a few miles east of Willcox. There, inside a cave, they found two saddles and two sets of bridles. Given the layer of dust on the items, they had clearly lain there for a long time. Others who have attempted to reconstruct the flight of Wheeler and George following the Willcox train robbery learned that the bandits rode south for a short distance and then turned east toward the Dos Cabezas. Their trail, according to some, led to Lion's Cave near the mountain range, a known hideout for outlaws. Some have speculated that the bulk of the $84,000 heist is cached nearby. As far as anyone knows, it has never been found.

CHAPTER 6

PEACH SPRINGS, FEBRUARY 8, 1897

James Fleming Parker, also known as Fleming Jim Parker and James T. Parker, was born in 1865 in Visalia, California, to a poor and troubled family. When he was ten years old, his mother died. Four years later his father committed suicide. Several months following that tragedy, Parker, only fifteen years old, was caught stealing cattle. He was tried, found guilty, and sentenced to a term in San Quentin State Prison. After his release, he found work as a cowhand in California and Arizona. He was later arrested for burglary, tried, and found guilty. He was sentenced to prison once again. Following his second release, he returned to Arizona to work as a ranch hand.

While in Arizona, Parker became friends with George Ruffner, who later became a noted lawman. During his time with Ruffner, it has been written, Parker helped organize the Prescott rodeo in July 1888. The Prescott Chamber of Commerce claims this was the first professional rodeo ever held in the United States.

Around this time, two of Parker's horses wandered onto the railroad tracks and were struck and killed by a train. Parker petitioned the railroad for compensation for his lost stock but was paid only a pittance. At least one western history writer is convinced that this episode led Parker to consider robbing a train to get even.

James Fleming Parker

On February 8, 1897, Parker, along with a companion, stopped the overland Santa Fe No. 1 train at a location called Rocky Cut, about six miles east of Peach Springs, Arizona. Once the train was stopped, Parker and his friend, both wearing masks, ordered engineer William Daze and the fireman out of the locomotive cab and back down the track and forced them to uncouple the express and mail cars from the rest of the train. Parker's companion carried several sticks of dynamite in his coat pockets.

When the train was stopped, express car messenger Alexander Summers, along with his assistant, slid the car door open and climbed to the ground. Before exiting the car, Summers retrieved his revolver from the desk, a Colt .45. As the two messengers lingered around the express car, they caught the attention of Parker's companion, who pointed his shotgun at them. Before he could pull the trigger, Summers aimed his revolver and fired a bullet into the outlaw's head, killing him instantly.

Standing next to the engineer and fireman, Parker watched his companion fall. Manifesting no emotion whatsoever, Parker turned to Daze and ordered him to climb into the locomotive and pull the train ahead two miles. This done, Parker instructed Daze to stop the train near Nelson Siding. When the train was halted, Parker marched the engineer and fireman back to the express car. With Summers and his assistant afoot far back on the tracks, Parker met no resistance as he entered the express car. Aware that he would find a locked safe, Parker had brought dynamite with which to blow it open. Unfortunately, the dynamite was in the possession of his dead companion two miles back.

Disappointed at not being able to blow open the express company safe, Parker exited the car and walked back to the mail car. Albert Grant was employed as the mail clerk. When Parker arrived and announced his intentions, Grant offered no resistance; he merely opened the mail car door and stepped back. Parker searched the car, grabbing several sacks of registered mail in the process. When he had all he could carry, he jumped to the ground and ran to his horse, which was tethered nearby. Moments later he was out of sight.

On returning to Peach Springs, engineer Daze provided an account of the robbery and a somewhat limited description of the bandit as Parker had worn a mask the entire time. Law enforcement authorities immediately deduced that the bandit was the man they knew as Fleming Jim Parker. Lawmen were also aware of his criminal record and of the time he had spent in prison. The body of the dead man was recovered but never identified.

On arriving at the site of the robbery, the sheriff's posse found the tracks of Parker's horse. For three days they doggedly pursued the robber, at times coming within rifle shot of him. On one occasion several shots were exchanged, but no one was hit. On the evening of the third day of the pursuit, a snowstorm forced the lawmen to abandon the chase.

As soon as the weather cleared, another posse was formed. Coconino County sheriff Ralph Cameron led this one to somewhat greater success than the previous. Among the posse members were two Indian trackers who had worked with Cameron on earlier manhunts. In a short time they came upon Parker's horse and saddle near a cabin outside Peach Springs. Cameron deduced that Parker had ridden his own horse to a point of fatigue and stolen another. Cameron also deduced that the outlaw was only a couple hours ahead. Since the Indian trackers had ponies better equipped to travel in the rugged country of this part of Arizona, Cameron sent them ahead to overtake Parker and attempt to capture him.

As the sun was going down, the Indians encountered Parker, subdued him, and tied him up. By this time it was dark, and the trackers decided to make camp at that point and return their prisoner to Cameron in the morning. During the night, however, Parker slipped his bonds. He picked up one of his captors' rifles, woke the Indians up, and ordered them out of the camp. During the night, both Parker's horse and those of the Indians had wandered away, and all three men were on foot. The Indians walked off in the direction of Peach Springs, while Parker set out in the opposite direction.

Having been employed as a cowhand for much of his life, Parker was unused to traveling anywhere for long on foot. After walking across the rugged and rocky landscape for two days, he was exhausted and lame. On the morning of February 15, as he was attempting to wade Diamond Creek twenty miles north of Peach Springs, Sheriff Cameron and his posse caught up with him. Parker offered no resistance and in fact appeared relieved to have been found. He had not eaten in two days, his feet were a mass of blisters, and he was suffering from exposure.

Parker was arrested and transported to the county jail at Prescott, ninety miles to the southeast. There, he was identified by the clerk, Grant, as the man who had robbed the mail car. Parker remained in the jail until his trial date. He decided not to wait. On May 9, he, along with two fellow prisoners, overpowered their jailer and escaped. From the jailer they retrieved a revolver. As they fled from the jail, they shot Erasmus Lee Norris, the assistant district attorney. Norris died that night. The three escapees raced for the prison livery stable, saddled horses, and rode away into the nearby hills. By sheer coincidence, the gelding stolen by Parker belonged to his old friend, Sheriff George Ruffner.

Two weeks later, a posse rode up on Parker as he was sleeping alongside a trail sixty miles north of Tuba City near the Utah border. He was rearrested with no difficulty and returned to Prescott, where he was charged with the murder of Norris. He was found guilty and sentenced to hang.

On the evening before his execution, Parker asked his friend Ruffner for a favor. Parker was acquainted with a lady of the evening named Flossie, who worked the cribs on Whiskey Row in Prescott. He asked Ruffner to arrange for him to spend the rest of the night with the woman. Ruffner made the necessary arrangements.

The criminal career of James Fleming Parker came to an end in June 1898. He was escorted up the gallows stairs by Ruffner. There, he shook hands with his old friend, as well as the hangman and jailer. Parker asked the jailer to tell the other prisoners that he "died game and like a man." A moment later, Ruffner placed a black hood over the head of the condemned. This done, Ruffner stepped aside, and the hangman pulled the lever, opening the trap door under Parker, who died instantly.

James Fleming Parker was buried in Citizens Cemetery in Prescott. Sheriff Ruffner drove the hearse that carried the luckless train robber to his grave.

CHAPTER 7

BURT ALVORD

Outside Arizona, the name Burt Alvord is little known, but during his careers in law enforcement and outlawry, he gained a reputation as a tough, determined, devious, and dangerous man. He lacked the charm, charisma, and loyalty of Jesse James, Butch Cassidy, and other noted train robbers and as a result garnered few newspaper headlines and precious little attention over the years from outlaw historians and enthusiasts.

This cunning train robber was born Albert W. Alvord to Charles E. and Lucy Alvord in Plumas County, California, on September 11, 1867. Father Charles, originally from New York, arrived in California to prospect for gold. Though he put in long hours and worked as hard as any man, he had little success. Realizing he was not cut out to be a gold miner, Charles Alvord sought and found steady employment as a mechanic for several mining companies. In time, he ran for public office and was elected constable and justice of the peace in the various towns and communities where he resided. In 1879, the Alvord family left California and moved to Pima County, Arizona. Following a short stay there, they moved to the mining town of Tombstone in Cochise County.

Young Burt Alvord had little to no formal education, but he watched and learned much from his father's handling of cases as a constable and justice of the peace. As he grew into manhood, Alvord developed a fondness for alcohol and was frequently seen

Burt Alvord

drinking in saloons. He also had a penchant for fisticuffs, was known never to back down, and often went looking for fights. Despite this somewhat reckless lifestyle, Cochise County sheriff John Slaughter hired nineteen-year-old Burt Alvord as a deputy in 1886. During this period, Alvord was described as intemperate, narrow-minded, and selfish. He gained valuable lawman experience, however, as he assisted Slaughter in capturing or killing several cattle rustlers and other bad men during the three years he served as a deputy.

While a deputy, Alvord was unable to refrain from spending a considerable amount of time in saloons drinking, gambling, and fighting. Such activities generated a negative image of the sheriff's department and gave Slaughter ample reason to reprimand him. Insulted and angered at the rebuke, Alvord quit. Over the next several months he went on to find employment as a lawman in other Arizona towns, including Fairbank and Pearce. In 1896, he met and married Lola Ochoa. A short time later he purchased a ranch and appeared ready and eager to settle down and pursue life as a cattle rancher while working part-time as a deputy.

Two years following Alvord's marriage, his father died. It is unclear what effect this had on him, but he immediately resigned his position as deputy, left his wife and ranch, and embarked on a life of crime. Within weeks, Alvord undertook a search for and found Billy Stiles and "Three-Fingered Jack" Dunlop, two noted outlaws he had pursued as a lawman. With Stiles and Dunlop, along with others, Alvord formed a gang and immediately set about committing armed robberies throughout Cochise County.

Alvord and Stiles were captured following a robbery but escaped. Dissatisfied with the small amount of money acquired from robbing travelers and stores, Alvord began to set his sights on richer targets. After casting about, he decided that the big money lay in robbing trains. He began to make plans and soon decided on a target: a Southern Pacific train that stopped at Cochise Junction.

CHAPTER 8

COCHISE JUNCTION, SEPTEMBER 11, 1899

In 1899 Cochise Junction in southwestern Arizona's Cochise County was a brief stop on the Southern Pacific Railroad line. There, trains took on coal and water. Located ten miles southwest of Willcox, Cochise Junction, now called simply Cochise, boasted a population of three thousand. Today less than fifty people reside in the community. Though virtually unknown to most residents of Arizona today, this seemingly insignificant railroad stop was the site of a daring train robbery that involved the sheriff of Willcox as well as three additional well-known residents of the town.

During the night of September 11, 1899, as a westbound Southern Pacific train was taking on water, two men hiding behind the small wooden station donned masks, approached the engine, and climbed aboard. At gunpoint, they ordered the engineer and fireman to uncouple the Wells, Fargo express car from the rest of the train. The express car was located behind the coal tender, which was directly behind the engine. This done, the bandits instructed the engineer to pull the shortened train forward approximately one mile before stopping. Once the train was halted, the two men forced open the door to the express car and climbed inside.

While one of the outlaws stood guard over the frightened express messenger, the other tied several sticks of dynamite to a large iron safe. After he lit the fuse, the outlaws and the messenger climbed out of the car. Moments later the explosion had blown

35

the door completely off the safe. Climbing back inside the express car, the robbers gathered up $30,000 worth of recently minted and uncirculated gold coins and placed them into two canvas bags. The robbers then carried the sacks to their horses, tied them on, and rode away into the night. While terrified, neither the engineer, the fireman, nor the express car messenger was harmed.

Once the train robbers were out of sight, the engineer backed the locomotive to Cochise Junction and recoupled it to the passenger coaches. As he did so, the fireman ran into the station to telegraph law enforcement authorities but found that the wires had been cut. A few more minutes passed before they located a nearby resident who agreed to ride to Willcox to inform the sheriff of the robbery.

At least one writer has identified Burt Alvord as the sheriff at the time. Others refer to him as a deputy sheriff and still others as a constable. Whatever his position, Alvord, on being informed of the train robbery, lost no time in forming a posse. On arriving at the scene of the robbery, however, he determined that the train robbers had left no tracks and that he was unable to pursue.

Within a few weeks of the robbery of the Southern Pacific train, area residents had forgotten the incident for the most part when a development occurred. An uncirculated gold coin had been used to purchase drinks at a Willcox saloon. A sharp-eyed bartender noticed the coin and, believing it to be related to the recent train robbery, alerted Wells, Fargo detectives as well as the Arizona Rangers. The coin was subsequently identified as part of the stolen loot.

The detectives and Rangers moved through town asking questions. Eyewitnesses came forth and identified a local barfly and ne'er-do-well named Bob Downing as the man who had passed the coin. Downing, however, denied any knowledge of the incident and said that he had been playing poker with Burt Alvord on the night of the train robbery. Initially, it appeared that Downing had an airtight alibi, but Ranger Burt Grover remained suspicious and decided to probe further.

Grover learned that the poker game had taken place in Schweitzer's Saloon. In addition to Downing and Alvord, two others were involved: Matt Burts and Billy Stiles. Downing, Burts, and Stiles occasionally served as deputies and sometimes as Alvord's bodyguards. Willcox residents regarded all three men as thugs and bullies. It is believed that Downing once rode with noted Texas train robber Sam Bass.

Ranger Grover harbored suspicions of all four of the poker players. After studying them for a time, he identified Stiles as the weakest of the quartet and decided to concentrate his efforts on him. Pulling Stiles aside one evening, Grover told him that he knew that the four were involved with the robbery of the Southern Pacific train and that Alvord and Downing were planning on blaming the crime on him. After placing him under arrest, Grover told him his companions planned on killing him. Frightened, Stiles confessed and explained how the robbery and the alibi had been arranged. On the night of the poker game, Stiles and Burts had slipped out the back door of Schweitzer's Saloon, robbed the train, and returned. The only person who saw the two men leave the game was a waiter, whom Alvord subsequently bribed or threatened.

Grover met with the other Rangers as well as the Wells, Fargo detectives, and plans were made to arrest the other three men. Burts departed Willcox before he could be apprehended, but Downing and Alvord were captured and transported to the jail in Tombstone. By this time, Stiles realized he had been duped and grew resistant to the authorities. He refused to sign a confession and informed the lawmen he would not testify against Alvord and Downing.

Grover had another idea. He arranged to have Downing released and planned to have him followed to see if he would lead authorities to the rest of the loot. Suspicious, Downing did no such thing. Alvord remained in jail, where Wells, Fargo detectives interrogated him and promised him a light sentence if he told them where the gold coins were hidden. They made the same offer to Stiles. Stiles led the detectives to believe that he would cooperate but wanted to think about the proposal for a few days.

Stiles had other plans in mind. On April 8, 1900, he and Alvord escaped from the Tombstone jail. In the process, twenty-four other prisoners were freed. Alvord and Stiles rode throughout Cochise County, stealing cattle and committing robberies. Wasting little time, they made plans to undertake another train robbery.

The robbery of the Southern Pacific train near Cochise Junction was the last reported successful train holdup in Arizona.

CHAPTER 9

FAIRBANK, FEBRUARY 15, 1900

Today Fairbank, Arizona, is a ghost town located near the San Pedro River, fifteen miles northeast of Sierra Vista. Named for railroad financier Nathaniel Kellogg Fairbank and established in 1881, the town was the rail stop nearest to the town of Tombstone. For a time it was regarded as important in the development of southeastern Arizona. In addition, Fairbank served as an important supply point for the numerous freighters hauling ore from the mines at Tombstone to the mills at Contention City and Charleston. The town at one point boasted a population of one hundred residents, a Wells, Fargo office, a meat market, a mercantile, and a stagecoach station.

On February 15, 1900, Fairbank was the site of an unusual train robbery attempt. On this evening, the Southern Pacific train pulled into the station as part of its normal stop on the Benson-Nogales run. Passengers disembarked and milled around the station platform, smoking and visiting, while packages from the express car were unloaded.

Suddenly, seven men bent on robbing the express car appeared on the platform among the passengers. Most researchers believe the leader of the gang was Burt Alvord and that he was accompanied by Three-Fingered Jack Dunlop, Bravo Juan Yoas, Billy Stiles, Bob Brown, and two brothers named Owen. Both Alvord and Stiles had been deputy sheriffs of Cochise County. Working as the express car messenger on this night was Jeff Milton, substituting for another agent who was too sick to make the run. By 1900, Milton had experienced a number of adventures, most of them relating to his work as a lawman. At fifteen, he lied about his age and enlisted in the Texas Rangers. After serving four years, he traveled to New Mexico and found work as a deputy US marshal. For a time in the 1880s, he served as a deputy under Cochise County sheriff John Slaughter. During this period, Milton became a veteran of several manhunts and shootouts. Later, Milton served as chief of police in El Paso, Texas.

From the express car, Milton heard someone from the platform shout, "Hands up!" Initially, he though a joke was being played on him. A moment later someone approached the express car and yelled for him to raise his hands and come out. A second later a shot was fired, the bullet knocking the hat from Milton's head. Milton reached for his revolver but suddenly remembered he had left it on a table deep inside the express car. Near the door where he stood, however, leaned a sawed-off shotgun. Milton was tempted to grab it and return fire but feared hitting some of the passengers.

Another shot from one of the robbers struck Milton in the left arm, shattering the bone. In pain, he dropped to the floor of the car. One of the bandits, believing the messenger was dead, approached the door. On his back, Milton reached for the shotgun. When the outlaws stepped inside the car, he fired. Eleven shotgun pellets hit Dunlop. Another pellet struck Yoas, who had come alongside his companion. Dunlop fell to the floor of the car, writhing in pain. Complaining that he had been wounded, Yoas left the platform and ran toward his horse.

Milton was bleeding badly from the wound to his arm, as the bullet had severed an artery. Desperate, he improvised a tourniquet that managed to stanch the blood flow somewhat. Then Milton pulled the keys to the express car safe from his pocket and tossed them into a pile of packages located at the far end of the

Jeff Milton

car. A moment later, Alvord and the rest of the bandits entered and searched Milton's pockets but found no keys. As Alvord was preparing to shoot Milton again, the train's engineer arrived and intervened, arguing that he was already dead. The bandits inspected the safe and quickly realized they would not be able to open it without a key. Angered, they fired several rounds from their rifles at the walls and ceiling of the express car. Having vented their frustration, they picked up Dunlop and made their way out of the car, off the platform, and to their horses, which were tied up a short distance away.

Milton, no stranger to shootouts, thwarted the train robbery attempt, but for the moment his own life was in danger as he continued to bleed out. He was tended to by crewmen and passengers who finally succeeded in stopping the blood loss. The railroad dispatched a special engine and boxcar to carry the now weakened and delirious Milton to the hospital at Tucson. There, Dr. H. W. Fenner tied the shattered bone together with piano wire. Two days later, when it became apparent that this method was insufficient, Milton was transported to San Francisco, California, where he was examined at the Southern Pacific Hospital. The doctors agreed that the arm needed to be amputated, but Milton refused. He enlisted a friend to take him to the office of Dr. George E. Goodfellow across town. Goodfellow cleaned out the wound and patched the arm back together, but informed Milton that the limb would be useless for the rest of his life. The physician was correct; Milton was never able to use the disabled arm. Following the treatment provided by Goodfellow, Milton's left arm ended up two to three inches shorter than the right. Unable to work, Milton retired to Tombstone. For a time he worked for the US Immigration Service as a border rider. Later, he moved to Tucson, where he stayed for the remainder of his life. He died on May 7, 1947, at the age of eighty-five.

Three-Fingered Jack Dunlop never recovered from the shotgun blast he received from Milton. Several days following the attempted robbery at Fairbank, the outlaw died from his wounds.

After escaping from the Fairbank train robbery debacle, Burt Alvord went into hiding for a time. Late in 1900, he was captured, taken to Tombstone, and placed in the town jail. Learning that his old friend was locked up, Billy Stiles rode to Tombstone, observed the comings and goings at the jail, and when he thought the time was right, broke Alvord out. In the process, a deputy was wounded and Stiles released another twenty-four prisoners.

In 1902, in exchange for a reduced sentence and a share of the reward money, Alvord surrendered to the Arizona Rangers to assist them in the pursuit and capture of Mexican bandit Augustine Chacon. Chacon was caught, tried, convicted, and hung. When it came time for Alvord to serve his sentence, he regretted making the promise and escaped again, this time in the company of Billy Stiles. The two men returned to their criminal ways and were, ironically, pursued by the same Arizona Rangers Alvord had previously assisted.

The two outlaws were captured again in 1903 but escaped a short time later. Alvord, anxious for relief from pursuit, sent the bodies of two dead Mexicans to Tombstone with a note indicating they were Alvord and Stiles. The ruse was quickly discovered, and pursuit was undertaken with renewed enthusiasm. The two men were tracked to the Mexican town of Naco in February 1904. A shootout ensued, with Alvord and Stiles suffering wounds. Outnumbered and outgunned, they surrendered.

Alvord was sentenced to two years in the Yuma prison. After his release, he traveled to Central America. The last record of his activities there indicates he had found employment working on the Panama Canal. Following that, no account of his whereabouts has ever been found. Alvord simply disappeared and was never heard from again. Alvord Road in Tucson was named for the former lawman and outlaw.

Fairbank ceased to be an important train and freight wagon stop when the silver mines around Tombstone played out. The town was soon abandoned. Today, it is listed on the official Ghost Town Trails and Tombstone Territory Map of Cochise County.

COLORADO

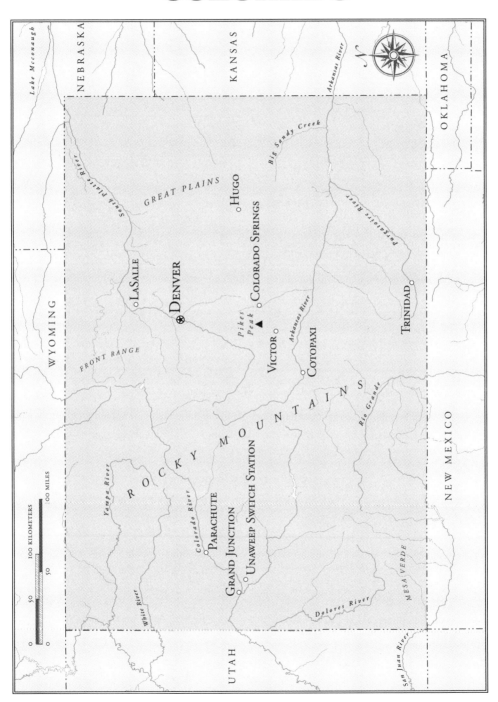

CHAPTER 10

COLORADO SPRINGS, OCTOBER 1881

The first recorded train robbery in the state of Colorado took place a few miles north of Colorado Springs in El Paso County in 1881. The money taken represented the largest train heist in the history of the state.

A Colorado and Southern Railroad train had just left the station at Colorado Springs, headed north toward Denver, when the engineer was forced to pull to a stop as a result of a barricade of railroad ties stacked on the tracks. No sooner had the train come to a halt when three masked men ran up to the locomotive from the shadows of the nearby trees and instructed the engineer and fireman to raise their hands and step out of the cab. Once on the ground, the two railroad employees were forced to lead the way back to the Wells, Fargo express car.

The train robbers called to the messenger inside the express car, who refused to answer. After the second attempt with no results, the robbers told the engineer to instruct the messenger to open the door. The engineer approached and begged the messenger to open up as failure to do so would result in harm or death to himself and the fireman.

As the engineer tried to convince the messenger to open the door, the conductor, curious as to what was going on, stepped down from one of the passenger coaches and started toward the express car. He was accompanied by several passengers. On spotting the newcomers, the robber fired a volley of shots toward the oncoming crowd, sending all back to the coach. The gunfire frightened the messenger, who thought the engineer and fireman were being killed. Concerned that he might be next if he resisted, he quickly opened the door.

As the messenger stood aside, the robbers scrambled into the express car. One of them carried a bundle of dynamite. Within minutes, it was attached to the safe and the fuse lit. The resulting explosion blew open the door to the safe, and the bandits withdrew $105,000 in cash and an estimated $40,000 worth of jewelry. Cash and jewelry were stuffed into canvas bags carried along for that purpose. The robbery of the express car was conducted efficiently and effectively and appeared to be well planned. Looking around the express car for anything else of value, here and there the robbers found and pocketed watches and more jewelry. This done, they jumped to the ground, tied the bags to the horses tethered nearby, and rode away toward the north.

The engineer and fireman raced back to the locomotive and returned the train to Colorado Springs. There, law enforcement authorities were alerted, and word of the robbery was communicated throughout the region. A posse was formed and raced to the site of the robbery. The lawmen followed the bandits' trail for several miles to a point where they had clearly replaced their mounts with fresh horses. The tracks proceeded toward the northwest into the mountains, but where the outlaws traversed the rocky slope, the posse lost the trail. The lawmen returned to Colorado Springs.

Not long after the holdup of the Colorado and Southern train, the robbers were identified as George Tipton, Oscar Witherill, and Gene Wright. It was also learned that the outlaws had crossed the Colorado portion of the Rocky Mountains, made their way into Idaho, and then turned south into Utah. Near the town of Corinne, the trio made a temporary camp and, while there, buried a significant portion of the train robbery loot. The cache is believed to be located on the bank of the Bear River where the stream forms a bend "against a low-timbered hill."

Carrying a few hundred dollars with them into the town of Corinne, the outlaws undertook a celebration of their newfound fortune. During this time, Corinne was a supply center for area miners and prospectors as well as ranchers and soldiers. Between the saloons and whorehouses, it didn't take the three train robbers long to run out of money. Finding their funds low, Witherill attempted to pawn a watch taken from one of the packages from the express car. The clerk who provided some small amount of money to Witherill for the watch became suspicious and alerted the town marshal, who had had his eye on the strangers for several days.

The marshal decided to confront the three men. In response, Witherill and Wright pulled their revolvers, and a brief gunfight ensued. During the melee, Tipton, who was standing several yards away, was wounded in the leg. Witherill and Wright were subdued and marched to the town jail. Tipton was ignored.

In an attempt to bargain, Wright and Witherill admitted their part in the robbery and told of burying most of the loot near the Bear River but refused to provide precise directions. The two men were made to stand trial, found guilty, and sentenced to the prison at Cañon City. Tipton, who apparently went unnoticed throughout the ordeal, remained in Corinne. He had decided to wait for his wound to heal and then travel to the Bear River to retrieve the remainder of the loot.

Unfortunately, Tipton's wound did not heal properly, and a serious infection required that the leg be amputated. As he recovered from his surgery, Tipton learned that the town marshal, along with railroad detectives, had him under observation. Fearing he would be arrested and sent to prison for robbery of the Colorado and Southern train, he fled the town one night. He decided to travel to Idaho to wait for his leg to heal and then return to the Bear River. Unfortunately, another infection set in. As Tipton crossed the border into Idaho, he spotted a ranch house and sought help. The rancher, Lafe Roberts, quickly determined that what was left of Tipton's leg was gangrenous. Two days later the outlaw was dead.

Before Tipton died, he told Roberts about the buried loot. Convinced the tale of a great amount of money cached in a sandy bank near the Bear River was the product of a dying man's delirium, Roberts thought little of it. Years later, however, on learning of Tipton's connection to the robbery of the Colorado and Southern train, he decided to go search for the treasure. Recalling the vague directions provided him by the dying Tipton, Roberts traveled to the Bear River. Before leaving home, he told several acquaintances about his quest. Word eventually spread throughout the area, and Roberts's activities soon drew the attention of Wells, Fargo officials, who retained an active file on the Colorado Springs train robbery. They located the rancher and questioned him but learned nothing. Either Roberts had little to tell the officials or simply remained closemouthed about the possible location of the robbery loot. Whatever the case, most are convinced that Roberts never found the cache.

Finding the Bear River train robbery loot has been the objective of both professional and amateur treasure hunters over the decades. Numerous forays into the Bear River area have been made and hundreds of holes dug into the banks. Maps purporting to show the location of the cache have been passed around, but none have ever been authenticated. To date no recovery has been reported. The search continues.

CHAPTER 11

UNAWEEP SWITCH STATION, NOVEMBER 3, 1887

The four outlaws who held up the Denver and Rio Grande (D&RG) passenger train at Unaweep Switch Station on November 3, 1887, had thoroughly planned the first part of the operation, the stopping of the train and the looting of the express and mail car. The second part of the robbery—the escape—did not go nearly as well, and their lack of preparation eventually spelled their doom.

The engineer for the D&RG passenger train had pulled out of the station at Grand Junction, Colorado, and was gradually picking up speed, heading southeast toward the next stop at the town of Delta, when he spotted a jumble of rocks piled on the track ahead. Since the locomotive sported a substantial cowcatcher on the front, the engineer at first believed plowing through the obstruction would be easy. On second thought, however, since the blockade was on a particularly tricky curve, and because he was transporting coaches filled with passengers, he decided to apply the brakes. It was 3:45 a.m., and the temperature was below freezing.

No sooner had the train stopped than a gunman appeared out of the darkness pointing a revolver at the engineer. At the same time, three additional robbers approached the mail car and were poised just outside the door, handguns ready. Inside the mail car, railway service clerk H. W. Grubb had just settled into a comfortable position, looking forward to the long nap he anticipated before arriving at the next stop. Jolted awake when the engineer suddenly halted the train, Grubb thought they had pulled into the station at Delta. It seemed far too early to be stopping, but the dutiful Grubb grabbed the mail pouch intended for Delta and slid open the mail car door in order to toss it onto the station platform. Instead of the station, Grubb saw a wide expanse of Colorado landscape as well as Unaweep Switch Station not far away. Unaweep Switch Station was only five miles east of Grand Junction. Grubb also saw three men wearing masks pointing weapons at him. Glancing toward the front of the train, Grubb spotted the engineer and fireman climbing down from the locomotive at gunpoint.

One of the train robbers asked Grubb if anyone else was in the mail car. When he replied that there wasn't, the gunman ordered him to go to the end of the car and stand facing the wall. Grubb complied. The three masked men climbed inside and began rummaging through the mail pouches. When they encountered registered mail, they took it.

From the end the mail car, Grubb, who was in shirtsleeves and shivering, complained that he was cold and requested that he be allowed to put on his coat. One of the outlaws checked the pockets for weapons and then tossed it to the clerk. A few minutes later the robbers had finished going through the mailbags and ordered Grubb to climb out of the car and join the engineer and fireman. Grubb hastened to do so. After Grubb departed, the three outlaws jumped from the mail car and walked down to the one behind it, the express car.

By this time, the express messenger, Dick Williams, had ascertained that a robbery was taking place, and he was determined to resist any effort to break into the express car for which he had been given responsibility. He readied for such by arming himself with a shotgun and revolver. When the outlaws arrived at the door of the express car and shouted for the messenger to open up, Williams said that he was unable to do so because a number of shipping trunks were stacked up against it. He suggested that the robbers go around to the door on the other side of the car. As the robbers did so, Williams peeked through a small window at the end of the car so he could see how many men he was up against. In the dark, however, he could not see them.

Once on the opposite side of the express car, the robbers again shouted for the messenger to open the door. When Williams made no move to do so, one of the men informed him they were going to use dynamite to blow the car up. At this threat, Williams decided opening the door was the prudent course of action, which he did a moment later.

On climbing into the express car, the robbers spotted two safes: the local and the express. The local safe, also called the messenger's safe, could be added to or subtracted from at every stop. The express safe was a through safe whose contents were intended for some destination farther down the line such as a bank or express company. At gunpoint, Williams opened the local safe, but inside the robbers found only $150. When they ordered Williams to open the express safe, the messenger explained that he was unable to do so, that it could only be opened by specified agents in the larger towns and cities encountered down the line, and that only they knew the combination.

Angered by this response, one of the robbers pointed his revolver at Williams's head and ordered him to open the safe or he would kill him. For several minutes Williams pleaded and explained that it was not in his power to open the safe. Just when Williams was convinced that he was going to be killed, the leader of the train robbers stepped forward and told the others to leave the messenger alone, that he was probably telling the truth. The robbers turned their attention to the rest of the shipments inside the express car. After snagging a couple of promising-looking packages and some COD letters, they returned to the mail car and went through it a second time in hopes of finding something valuable.

As the robbery progressed, the conductor, who had realized what was transpiring, moved through the coaches attempting to calm the passengers. He explained that a robbery was taking place but that the outlaws would likely be interested only in the contents of the mail and express cars. One of the passengers was a nervous gentleman from Scotland who was touring America. Severely distressed by the potential of being harmed, he recalled reading somewhere that the outlaws of the American West never robbed or hurt female passengers. The Scotsman grabbed a suitcase from a nearby female passenger, rummaged through it until he found a dress, and was in the act of putting it on as a disguise when the conductor stepped in and forced him to calm down, telling him that his ruse would not work. The dress was returned.

As the train robbers were gathering up their booty and pre-paring to depart, the brakeman and a passenger approached the mail car with the notion that they might be of some assistance. On spotting them, the outlaws fired shots in their direction, sending them back into hiding. For a time, the robbers debated whether to enter the coaches and rob the passengers; instead they decided that they had spent too much time with the train and needed to escape. After climbing out of the mail car, they hastened to their horses, which were tied nearby. Mounting up, they rode off into the darkness.

After the robbery had been reported, the D&RG Express Company offered a reward of $3,000 for the capture of the perpe-trators. The US government added $1,000 to that amount. In all it seemed like an impressive reward, considering the small amount of cash and other valuables that the robbers took. The large reward was presumably offered in an effort to dissuade further attempts at train robberies. For 1887, $4,000 was a substantial sum of money. The amount attracted one of the most effective and efficient man hunters in Colorado at the time, Cyrus Wells "Doc" Shores. At the time, Shores was the sheriff of Gunnison County. To assist him, Shores enlisted the services of his brother-in-law, M. L. Allison.

Shores and Allison arrived at Unaweep Switch Station and the scene of the robbery on the following day. It was their intention to

Cyrus Wells "Doc" Shores

locate and follow the tracks of the bandits, but the area had been trampled over by the Mesa County posse that raced to the site on learning of the robbery. Undeterred, Shores and Allison rode in ever-widening circles around the site for a full day but found nothing. On a hunch, Shores decided to cross the nearby Gunnison River and look for tracks along the southwestern bank. After two days of searching, Shores found the tracks he believed he was looking for—horses heading in the direction of Bangs Canyon. He set out after them.

Bangs Canyon was a remote and wild cut in the mountain range southwest of the Gunnison River crossing. The canyon led to a plateau with an elevation of nine thousand feet. On the second day of following the tracks, Shores noted that the riders were joined by two more. He was now convinced that he was following the tracks of the Unaweep Switch Station train robbers.

Shores and Allison invested four days riding throughout the Bangs Canyon region before returning to Grand Junction. From there, they took the train to Gunnison, where they procured additional supplies and fresh horses. At Gunnison, James Duckworth, a special agent for the D&RG railroad company, joined the search team, as did Tom Denning, an area rancher who also possessed a stellar reputation as a man hunter. Together, the four men returned to the Bangs Canyon region and continued the search for the train robbers. Their hunt was hampered by the arrival of a blizzard. The snow covered the tracks they were following, and the freezing temperatures made for an uncomfortable search. Duckworth, unused to the rugged life of the western outdoors, fell ill, and Shores was forced to take him back to town. Allison and Denning traveled to Delta, a small town forty miles southeast of Grand Junction. The following day, Shores rejoined the two men there.

At Delta, the trackers obtained some information they felt might be helpful. A short time prior to the robbery, four men unknown to anyone in town had arrived on foot leading only one packhorse. They camped on the outskirts of the town and constructed a boat. When curious residents of Delta approached the men and inquired as to what they were up to, they explained that they were from Carbondale, seventy-five miles to the northeast, and used to work for the Colorado Midland Railroad. They identified themselves as Ed Rhodes, Bob Wallace, and Jack and Bob Smith.

Shores thought the arrival of the four strangers in the area more than a coincidence. He forwarded the information to the office of the Pinkerton National Detective Agency in Denver and requested information on the four men, suggesting that the names might possibly be aliases. As Shores was preparing to renew the search for the train robbers, Denning took sick and was forced to return to his home.

With all the setbacks, Shores was growing discouraged. Just as he was considering abandoning the search, he received a report that four men matching the descriptions of those he was looking for had been spotted at Cisco, Utah, forty miles southwest of Grand Junction. When last seen, the four were boarding a train bound for Salt Lake City. Shores sent Allison, along with a Gunnison County deputy sheriff, there to see what they could find out. After conferring with city law enforcement officials, Allison received an offer of help. Three of the men were arrested the following day. The three gave their names as Ed Rhodes and Jack and Bob Smith. Following a brief interrogation, all three admitted their role in the Unaweep Switch Station train robbery.

On receiving word of the capture, Shores bought a ticket for the next train to Utah. Seldom in his career as a man hunter had he been put to such lengths. On meeting with the three train robbers, Shores admitted to them that they had caused him a number of difficulties. In turn, Rhodes told Shores that he was "the damndest bloodhound" he had ever seen. Rhodes admitted that the last several weeks on the run from the lawmen had been hard, that the outlaws had been freezing, starving, and living like wild animals. Jack Smith told Shores he was finally glad they got caught, that they had spent the entire time looking over their shoulders, not experiencing a warm day or a solid meal the entire time.

Under further questioning, Shores learned the identity of the fourth robber. The man who went by the alias Bob Wallace was in truth Bob Boyle from Paola, Kansas. Boyle was eventually tracked down at his job working on an irrigation canal near Price, Utah. Ignoring protocol related to warrants, Shores had Boyle arrested and returned to Colorado for trial. Each of the train robbers was found guilty and sentenced to time in prison.

As far as is known, the Unaweep Switch Station train robbery was the first for Rhodes, Boyle, and the Smith brothers, as well as the last. After serving their time, Bob Smith and Bob Boyle traveled to the Alaskan gold fields to try to make their fortune. Whatever success they may have had remains unknown. Following his release, Ed Rhodes found work in Boulder, Colorado. By all accounts he was a steady and reliable employee, but one day he fell into an argument with a fellow worker who shot and killed him. Jack Smith walked out of prison and, as soon as he was able, settled into a quiet life in the small town of Whitewater, Colorado, located a few miles east of Unaweep Switch Station.

Doc Shores was nicknamed for the doctor who delivered him. Before serving as the Gunnison County sheriff, Shores had worked as a cowhand, a bullwhacker, and a freighter. Later, he became a US deputy marshal, a railroad detective, and chief of police for Salt Lake City.

CHAPTER 12

COTOPAXI, AUGUST 31, 1891

Cotopaxi, Colorado, is a tiny community of less than fifty residents nestled in a picturesque canyon through which flows the Arkansas River. The nearest town of any consequence is Cañon City, thirty-three miles to the east. The town was named by Henry Thomas, an early prospector, for the Cotopaxi Volcano in Ecuador.

In 1882, Cotopaxi was established as a colony for sixty Russian Jewish immigrants. They planned to develop a farming community and to take advantage of the presumed benefits associated with the Homestead Act, which granted each male head of a family 160 acres of land. The immigrants were told that, on arrival, housing would be ready for them. When they finally landed at Cotopaxi, however, they found that only a few of the promised houses had been constructed. Many of the families were forced to spend the winter in nearby caves and hastily constructed rock-and-canvas shacks.

The new colonists also found themselves short of the supplies they needed to till the soil and plant their crops, mostly potatoes and corn. Unfortunately, late freezes killed most of their harvest. They also learned, belatedly, that the growing season lasted only four months of the year. As a result, the immigrants were forced to seek employment and found work with the Denver and Rio Grande (D&RG) Railroad, which paralleled the Arkansas River for several miles and was laying track over Marshall Pass to the west. The colony abandoned Cotopaxi in 1884.

On the night of August 31, 1891, a group of masked men forced a railroad employee to flag down the D&RG eastbound train four miles out of Cotopaxi. When the train pulled to a halt, the robbers forced the engineer and fireman out of the locomotive cab and back to the mail car, which the bandits broke into using heavy tools. After searching through the registered mail and finding nothing of value, the robbers turned their attention to the next car, a combined express and baggage car.

On arriving at the express car, the robbers again attempted to break in but were greeted by several shots from a revolver from the inside of the car. The messenger, A. C. Angell, who had discerned that a robbery was taking place when the train came to a stop in the remote location, armed himself and waited for the anticipated break-in. After emptying his revolver and neither striking a single robber nor dissuading the gang in the least, he surrendered and slid open the door.

There were seven robbers in all. While a few stood guard outside the express car, the remainder climbed inside and rummaged through its contents. They found the express company strongbox and broke it open—it yielded $3,600 in cash along with some gold bars. From the fireman they took a gold watch. Not wishing to rob the passengers, the outlaws retreated to their horses and rode away.

A short time later, law enforcement authorities were notified of the robbery and formed a posse. From the scene of the robbery, the outlaws had ridden away in the direction of West Mountain Valley (also printed as Wet Mountain Valley) along the eastern slope of the Sangre de Cristo Mountains. After following the tracks for several miles, the posse determined that the train robbers had ridden among a herd of cattle, thereby hiding their tracks. The posse decided to give up the pursuit, turned, and rode away.

Unhappy with the lack of effort by the local law enforcement, the D&RG officials sent two detectives from the Pinkerton National Detective Agency to Cotopaxi to investigate the robbery. This marked the beginning of a series of adventures to come for

Tom Horn

the two detectives. One of them was Tom Horn, who had joined the Pinkertons after a successful career as an army scout. Horn went on to become a noted western figure as a cowhand, range detective, soldier, and killer. As a hired gunman, he is reputed to have slain seventeen men.

The second detective was Cyrus Wells "Doc" Shores. Shores, a noted figure in western lawman history, had gained fame as a Gunnison County sheriff, a position wherein he earned a reputation as a dogged and successful man hunter. It took several months of dedicated detective work, but eventually Horn and Shores caught up with and arrested Ben Curtis and Robert "Pegleg" Eldridge at a farm near Washita in Indian Territory (today Oklahoma). A short time later, the rest of the gang was located and arrested. It included Frank Hallock, Tom McCoy, William Parry, and two brothers named Price. The seven men comprised what was known in the area as the McCoy Gang, which had been responsible for several robberies and livestock rustling incidents.

Parry broke under interrogation and confessed to the Cotopaxi train robbery. He also implicated the six other prisoners. Parry related that Curtis and Eldridge had masterminded the robbery of the D&RG train. The two men were tried separately in Denver, found guilty, and sentenced to prison at the Detroit House of Correction in Michigan. During the trials of the other outlaws, it was learned that Parry had earlier escaped from jail at Canon City. He was returned to serve out his term. The remaining prisoners were tried and eventually acquitted for "lack of evidence."

CHAPTER 13

LASALLE, AUGUST 17, 1892

Throughout the history of America's 180-plus train robberies, only a handful were thwarted by the heroic actions of an engineer, a conductor, or a brakeman. Rarely did passengers get involved. During the attempted robbery of a Denver Pacific passenger train near LaSalle (also seen as La Salle), Colorado, however, an unassuming young man new to the Rocky Mountain West took it upon himself to do battle with three masked and armed train robbers. His efforts resulted in the bandits abandoning the train.

S. J. Payne was described as "frail" and "dandified." He was employed by the Evans and Littlefield Company of Denver as a salesman. Payne was regarded as a fine employee and was eager to impress the officials at his company. Born and raised in the East, Payne was new to the West and confessed certain nervousness about traveling by train. His trepidation, he explained, was the result of the numerous train robberies he had read about in newspapers.

Fearful of encountering bandits and nervous about the possibility of getting shot, Payne purchased a small revolver and kept it on his person every time he traveled. He had never fired a weapon before, and he'd had no time to practice doing so before he was to leave for Cheyenne, Wyoming. When Payne stepped aboard the Denver Pacific passenger train at the Denver Station, little did he realize that he would soon have an opportunity to use the weapon.

As the train pulled out of the station, Payne settled deep into his seat for the long trip to Cheyenne. He intended to nap much of the distance. The next stop would be at LaSalle, forty-five miles away and just south of the town of Greeley. The stop was uneventful, and Payne continued to doze.

When the Denver Pacific railroad personnel had completed their tasks at the station, the engineer sounded the whistle and prepared to pull away. It was seventy-five more miles to Cheyenne, thought Payne, time enough for an extended slumber. His sleep was about to be interrupted, for as the train was picking up speed, three men wearing masks and brandishing revolvers entered the car. In loud voices, they informed the passengers that this was a robbery and instructed them to yield their money, watches, jewels, and other valuables immediately. To emphasize their orders, the robbers fired several shots into the ceiling of the car.

Women screamed and fainted, and men trembled as they reached for their wallets. Several of the passengers attempted to shove their money and watches under the seats, and others tried to hide under them. The robbers walked down the center aisle of the coach holding out canvas bags in which the passengers placed their valuables.

Payne was dozing at the opposite end of the car from which the robbers entered. Stirring from his sleep, it took him a few moments to come to understand that the train was being robbed. Payne's worst fears were being realized. As he considered the events, he noted that two of the robbers were making their way toward the rear of the coach where he was seated. Payne was determined not to be robbed.

Just as the two bandits came near his position, Payne withdrew his revolver from a light bag he carried, raised it, and began firing at the intruders. According to one of the passengers seated nearby, Payne began firing wildly at the outlaws, the bullets spraying in various directions. One of them, however, struck one of the robbers, who screamed and doubled over in pain. At this, the gang, not anticipating and surprised by the resistance, turned and ran out the front end of the coach. As the train was still moving along at a relatively slow speed, the three jumped to the ground. During their escape, they dropped the bags containing the items taken in the robbery. All of the money, watches, and jewelry were returned to the passengers.

The robbers were neither identified nor apprehended. Payne was regarded as a hero and celebrated by the passengers all the way to Cheyenne.

CHAPTER 14

VICTOR, MARCH 24, 1895

The Victor, Colorado, train robbery of 1895 was unique in the sense that the holdup was perpetrated by no less than a lawman who held an appointment as a federal marshal.

Victor, located twenty-five miles southwest of Colorado Springs, was founded in 1891 following the discovery of gold. The town was named after the Victor Mine, which was named after an early settler in the area, Victor Adams. During its mining heyday in the 1890s, Victor boasted a population in excess of eight thousand people. Today less than four hundred souls live in the town.

At 9:50 p.m. on the night of March 24, 1895, the Florence and Cripple Creek Railroad No. 60 train was pulling away from the Victor station when two men wearing masks dashed out from behind the building and raced toward the slow-moving train. One of them leapt aboard the blind on the baggage car just behind the tender, while the second climbed onto the platform of the Pullman sleeper.

After crawling across the top of the tender, the first bandit dropped into the locomotive cab, pointed a revolver at the engineer, and ordered him to pull the train to a stop at a selected point up ahead, 1.5 miles out of Victor. Just as the train halted, four additional masked men appeared out of the shadows and approached the locomotive. The robber in the cab told the engineer and fireman to remain quiet and unmoving until directed otherwise.

As the engineer and fireman were held at gunpoint, the robber who leapt aboard the sleeper car entered and began waking the passengers and ordering them to hand over their money and any items of value. When he had held up everyone in the sleeper car, he exited it and entered the coach and robbed all the passengers there. Though the robber was demanding and waved his handgun around, the passengers later stated he was "jovial." He, along with the rest of the robbers, was described as wearing "miner's clothes and slouch hats." When he had finished robbing all the passengers, he rejoined the rest of the gang. While one of them kept watch over the engineer and fireman, the rest walked down to the mail and express cars, entered them, and while keeping the messengers and clerks at bay with firearms, continued looting.

After the robbers had taken everything they thought had value, they climbed down and ordered the engineer to proceed southward toward the train's next stop at Florence, thirty miles away. Immediately on arrival, the conductor jumped from the train, ran into the building, and telegraphed area law enforcement authorities about the robbery.

Early the following morning, the Teller County sheriff organized a posse containing twelve members and set out for the robbery scene. On arriving, they could find no tracks. Refusing to give up, the sheriff telegraphed the police chief in Walsenburg and asked to borrow the department's bloodhound. The dog was shipped to Victor by a special train. Lawmen then carried the dog out to the robbery site and waited for it to pick up a trail. In the meantime, some two thousand Victor residents arrived at the scene to observe the goings-on. Before long, the bloodhound had picked up the robbers' scent, and the search got underway. It was joined by dozens of Victor citizens along with some residents from nearby Cripple Creek.

Late that same day, the bloodhound led the posse to a remote cabin in the mountains near the Strong Mine. Inside they found former deputy sheriff and federal marshal Bob Taylor and a seventeen-year-old youth named Frank Wallace. The two men were placed under arrest and transported to Cripple Creek. There, the conductor and brakeman identified Taylor as the man who went through the Pullman sleeper and the passenger car robbing people. Others identified young Wallace as the other robber. Following a brief trial, both men were found guilty and sentenced to prison.

CHAPTER 15

HUGO, AUGUST 4, 1900

Hugo was a service center for farming and ranching enterprises along the Big Sandy River in the eastern part of Colorado. From time to time a Union Pacific train would stop at the small Hugo station to take on a load of produce for distribution elsewhere.

Around midnight on August 4, 1900, the eastbound Union Pacific No. 4 passed through Hugo. In one of the Pullman coaches, the passengers were all asleep. The conductor, a man named Wilson, relieved at the calm that had spread through the coach, was himself enjoying a bit of a rest when he spotted two men riding the blind at the tail end of the car. Believing the men were hobos enjoying a free ride, Wilson rose from his seat to approach them. One of Wilson's responsibilities on the train was to remove illegal passengers.

When Wilson opened the car door and stepped onto the blind, the strangers, both wearing masks, pointed revolvers at him and ordered him back inside. One of the newcomers handed Wilson a sack and ordered him to walk down the aisle, wake the passengers, and instruct them to empty their pockets and place money and valuables into it. The first person who refused, stated one of the robbers, would be killed. Wilson did as he was ordered. One of the robbers stationed himself at the front of the car, the other at the rear.

As Wilson made his way between the seats, one of the outlaws ordered the passengers to rise from their seats and stand in the center of the aisle where they could be seen. When Wilson reached the last passenger, trouble started. The passenger was W. J. Fay, a sixty-six-year-old California resident who had spent most of his life as a prospector and miner. He had dealt with toughs in the past and had little patience with them. Instead of turning over his cash and watch to Wilson, Fay pulled out a revolver and pointed it at the robber standing nearby. The outlaw was prepared for such an event. Before Fay could pull the trigger, the robber raised his own handgun and shot him in the head. Fay fell out of his seat and into the aisle.

The robber at the other end of the car yanked the bell cord, causing the train to slow. When the speed had been considerably reduced, both robbers leaped from the blind to the ground and fled into the darkness.

Several hours later, just before sunrise, the train robbers stole two horses from a ranch at Boyero, twenty miles southeast of Hugo, and rode eastward toward the Kansas border. Around mid-morning, a posse from Hugo had arrived at the point along the tracks where the robbers leaped from the train. The lawmen were soon joined by a squad of several mounted Union Pacific agents who had arrived in a car specially equipped for transporting horses.

Meanwhile, the robbers rode their stolen horses hard. Before reaching the Kansas border, the two mounts could go no farther and dropped. A short time later, the bandits spotted two more horses in a nearby field and confiscated them. These, like the previous, were also ridden hard. When they could go no farther, the horses gave out and stopped. Hours later, the posse found them dead.

Unable to procure any additional horses, the robbers hopped aboard an eastbound Rock Island train. When the train slowed as it approached Goodland, Kansas, eighteen miles east of the Colorado line, they jumped off. The two men then made their way to a farmhouse they spotted in the distance. Walking up to the front door, the robbers identified themselves as "travelers" from Iowa who were on their way to California and requested permission to sleep in the barn. The family, named Bartholomew, welcomed the strangers and invited them to stay for dinner. Enjoying the relative safety of the Bartholomew farm, the two men decided to remain for a few days.

It did not take long for Sherman County sheriff William Walker to learn of the presence of the newcomers at the Bartholomew farm. Suspicious, Walker alerted officials of the Union Pacific Railroad. Walker, along with two deputies, dressed up as cowhands and rode out to the Bartholomew farm with a herd of horses to try to make some determination of the situation. A mile behind the deputies and out of sight, a posse of Union Pacific agents waited.

The two train robbers were out in one of Bartholomew's fields when the sheriff and the deputies rode toward the farmhouse. Suspicious about their arrival, the two men raced toward the house. When the lawmen spotted the suspects, they opened fire. They paused when the strangers shot back at them, one of their bullets wounding a deputy in the stomach. The second deputy returned fire, hitting one of the robbers in the head and killing him. The remaining train robber made it to the farmhouse, where he mounted a defense against his attackers. For the next couple of hours, both sides exchanged gunfire, with no one being struck.

The Bartholomew farm was close enough to town that residents could hear the gun battle taking place. Curious, dozens of them rode horses and wagons or traveled afoot to the location to witness the goings-on. Several brought their own weapons, and a few with rifles stationed themselves at convenient locations to shoot into the house at the gunman within.

Two hours before sunset, Sheriff Walker determined he had had enough of the standoff and decided to burn the train robber out. He located the Bartholomew family, explained his plan, and assured them that the county and the Union Pacific Railroad Company would cover the cost of rebuilding the house. The family agreed, and a few short minutes later the house was aflame.

Hours later, with the Bartholomew house burned to the ground, law enforcement officials walked among the ashes. They found the body of the gunman and determined he had committed suicide, shooting himself in the head, rather than be taken prisoner. In his pockets they found the two masks used in the holdup as well as a pocket watch taken from one of the passengers. The dead man was later identified as John Jones. The robber killed earlier was identified as his brother Jim Jones. No information on where they came from or where they lived was ever found.

CHAPTER 16

TRINIDAD, NOVEMBER 18, 1902

The Trinidad train holdup represented a stunning departure from what had come to be a standard procedure for robbing trains. In this instance, the express car messenger took unusual initiative and discouraged the bandits by attacking them and killing one.

It was a moonless night on November 18, 1902, when engineer John Guilfril of the Colorado and Southern No. 4 passenger train chugged northward toward the southeastern Colorado mining town of Trinidad. Guilfril had just brought the train over Raton Pass ten miles to the south and was looking forward to the extended break at the next stop. As Guilfril contemplated arriving at the station in the next few minutes, a swinging red lantern ahead on the tracks, a signal for caution, suddenly jerked him from his reverie. Guilfril slowed the train and attempted to discern what might be the problem ahead when a number of masked men appeared out of the dark and began shooting at the locomotive, forcing the engineer to halt the train.

Guilfril, along with the fireman, was ordered out of the cab and escorted down the tracks to the express car. When they arrived, the outlaws fired shots at the coaches to keep the passengers from exiting the cars and perhaps interrupting the robbery. While one of the outlaws held his revolver on Guilfril and the fireman, another crawled under the express car to set a dynamite charge. They intended to blow up the car, take what valuables they could find, and ride away.

Once the charge was set, one of the outlaws ordered Guilfril to climb under the car and light the fuse. Reluctant to help blow up part of the train for which he was responsible, the engineer was quickly persuaded by the threat of getting shot if he didn't. Guilfril tried several times to light the fuse, but the wind was blowing out the matches before they could be applied. One of the bandits, later identified as A. F. Hudson, grew frustrated at the delay, pushed Guilfril aside, and climbed under the car. Lying on his back half-way under the car, Hudson likewise had difficulty lighting the fuse.

As he was striking his third match, the express car messenger, H. W. Sherwick, suddenly slid the car door aside and appeared in the opening with a revolver in his hand and a defiant look in his eye. Spotting an outlaw half under his express car, Sherwick hesitated not at all and shot the robber in the stomach.

Stunned by this sudden turn of events, the remaining three outlaws turned and, leaving Hudson writhing in pain, ran for the nearby woods, where they had tied their horses. Moments later, Guilfril and Sherwick heard them galloping away. Hudson died the following day.

A posse was quickly formed and a search for the bandits undertaken, but no success was forthcoming. Other than Hudson, the foiled robbers were never identified. Hudson, as it turned out, was employed as a coal miner at nearby Gray Creek. Law enforcement authorities presumed that the three unidentified bandits were among Hudson's fellow miners, but a subsequent investigation yielded no results.

The Colorado and Southern Railroad regarded express car messenger Sherwick as a hero, though he resigned his position a short time later.

CHAPTER 17

HARVEY "KID CURRY" LOGAN

Harvey Logan is listed among the better-known outlaws in American history. Though he never gained the recognition accorded Billy the Kid, Jesse James, Butch Cassidy, and a few others, he was no less effective as an outlaw. A member of Cassidy's Wild Bunch, Logan was referred to as the "wildest of them all." During his criminal career, he took part in numerous train and bank robberies and several shootouts. He is reputed to have killed as least nine lawmen and two others.

Logan was born in Tama County, Iowa, in 1867. The exact date has never been established. Nine years later, when his mother died, Logan and three of his brothers were sent to Dodson, Missouri, to live with an aunt. Growing up, Logan took well to working on a farm and became adept at breaking horses. As soon as he was old enough to earn a living, he hired out to neighboring farmers and ranchers, eventually making his way to Rising Star, Texas, where he broke horses on the Cross L Ranch. There he met future train robber George "Flat Nose" Curry. Curry impressed Logan so much that he adopted his surname and was soon referred to as "Kid Curry."

Kid Curry and his brothers gained reputations as hard workers. Once they received their paychecks, they became hard partiers, sharing a passion for alcohol and prostitutes. Following a robbery, Logan would reportedly move in with prostitutes and drink until

Harvey Logan, aka Kid Curry

his money was gone. He also reportedly fathered eighty-five ille-gitimate children, though no proof exists. When sober, Logan was reputed to be well-mannered, likable, and a good worker.

Logan's path in life changed markedly in Montana when law-man Powell "Pike" Landusky accused him of seducing his daugh-ter, Elfie. Landusky filed assault charges, and Logan was arrested and severely beaten. Two of Logan's friends—A. S. Lohman and

Frank Plunkett—came up with a $500 bond for Curry's release. Landusky's daughter, Elfie, later admitted that she was having relations with Logan's brother Lonny.

Incensed by his treatment during the legal process, Logan vowed revenge. On December 27, 1894, he encountered Landusky in a saloon, attacked the lawman, and knocked him out. As Logan walked away, Landusky regained consciousness, yanked his revolver from the holster, and threatened his attacker, who was unarmed. As Landusky verbally abused Logan and renewed his threats, Jim Thornhill, a friend and a partner of Logan's brother in a mining venture, handed Kid Curry a revolver. Landusky aimed at his adversary and pulled the trigger, but his weapon jammed. Logan raised the handgun and shot Landusky dead.

Logan was arrested for the killing. An inquest found that he had acted solely in self-defense, and he was released. Later, however, a formal trial was scheduled, to be presided over by a judge who was a close friend of Landusky's. Logan decided not to wait around for the proceedings and fled.

A short time later, Logan joined up with Thomas "Black Jack" Ketchum's gang. Ketchum was a wanted train and stagecoach robber. As such, he soon attracted the attention of Pinkerton detectives hired to investigate train robberies. In January 1896, Logan received information that a friend of Landusky's, James Winters, had been observing him and was interested in the reward being offered for his arrest. Logan, accompanied by brothers Johnny and Lonny, confronted Winters. The subsequent argument erupted into a shootout. Johnny was killed, and Logan and Lonny fled.

Following another train robbery led by Black Jack Ketchum, a disagreement ensued over the division of the loot. Dissatisfied, Logan and his brother left the gang. In need of money, the two went to work for a circus. When the season for the circus ended, they found employment on a cattle ranch near Sand Gulch, Colorado, north of Cañon City. Around this time the Pinkerton agent trailing Logan lost track of him.

Later, Logan and brother Lonny formed a gang that included George "Flat Nose" Curry and Walt Putnam. Logan set out searching for potential train robbery opportunities. On April 15, 1897, Logan was in Powder River, Wyoming, and became involved in a disagreement with Deputy Sheriff William Deane. Deane was killed, and while there were no witnesses, most are convinced that Logan was the murderer. A short time later, Logan returned to work on the ranch at Sand Gulch.

In June 1897, Logan left his job as a cowhand and, accompanied by his gang, traveled to Belle Fourche, South Dakota, where they robbed the town's bank. As they fled the scene, a number of townsfolk fired on the gang. The robbers escaped, but one of them, Tom O'Day, was captured after the gunfire spooked his horse and he was left afoot. As Logan and the remainder of the gang were planning another robbery, a posse from Belle Fourche caught up with them in Fergus County, Montana. During the ensuing gunfight, Logan was shot through the wrist. As he attempted to escape, his horse was shot out from under him, and he was captured. Logan and two additional gang members—George Curry and Walt Putnam—were taken to the Deadwood, South Dakota, jail to await legal proceedings.

The outlaws did not wait long. At the first opportunity, they overpowered the jailer, escaped, and fled for Montana. Along the way, they robbed two post offices.

By the spring of 1899, Logan had become a member of Butch Cassidy's Hole-in-the-Wall Gang, also referred to as the Wild Bunch. On June 2, 1899, the gang robbed the Union Pacific Railroad Overland Flyer near Wilcox, Wyoming (see chapter 43). The robbers were identified, but all escaped and remained on the run.

A few days after the Wilcox train robbery, Kid Curry and/or Tom Roberts shot and killed Converse County sheriff Josiah Hazen. (Various newspaper accounts credited one or the other, with some even naming George Curry as the shooter.) Logan and his gang retreated to the Hole in the Wall hideout. Logan reportedly shared a cabin with Harry Longabaugh, known as the Sundance Kid.

Feeling the pressure of pursuit by lawmen, Logan, along with Butch Cassidy and other gang members, fled to Alma, New Mexico, where they found work on a ranch. While there, Logan took some time off to travel to Folsom, New Mexico, with gang members Elzy Lay and Sam Ketchum (brother to Black Jack Ketchum), where they robbed a Colorado and Southern train (see chapter 38). A posse led by Huerfano County, Colorado, sheriff Ed Farr caught up with the outlaws near Turkey Creek. For four days, lawmen and train robbers exchanged gunfire. Elzy Lay shot and killed Sheriff Farr and Colfax County deputy sheriff Henry Love. Lay received a wound, as did Sam Ketchum. Ketchum's wound proved fatal; he died several days later while in jail. Lay was captured and sentenced to life in prison for the killings. Logan escaped and fled to San Antonio, where he met Della Moore, a prostitute who also went by the aliases Annie Rogers and Maude Williams. Logan and Moore became lovers.

In February 1900, Logan and fellow gang member Bill Carver were in St. Johns, Arizona. Logan was paying his bills with money that was identified as having come from the Wilcox train robbery. Apache County sheriff Edward Beeler gathered a posse and set out to arrest Logan, catching up with him on March 28. Rather than be arrested, the two outlaws decided to shoot it out with the lawmen. The end result was the killing of deputies Andrew Gibbons and Frank LeSeur. Logan and Carver escaped.

On May 26, Logan rode into Moab, Utah. There, he encountered Grand County sheriff Jesse Tyler and Deputy Sam Jenkins. Tyler and Jenkins were members of the posse that killed brothers Lonny and George Curry. Logan shot and killed both lawmen. This done, he returned to the Hole in the Wall and rejoined Butch Cassidy and Wild Bunch.

On August 29, 1900, the gang, including Logan, robbed the Union Pacific No. 3 train near Tipton, Wyoming (see chapter 44).

Following this robbery, Logan and gang member Ben Kilpatrick fled to Fort Worth, Texas. By June, Logan was back at the Hole in the Wall. On July 3, 1901, the Wild Bunch, including Logan, robbed a Great Northern train near Wagner, Montana.

In December 1901, Logan was in Knoxville, Tennessee, where he engaged in a shootout with policemen William Dinwiddie and Robert Saylor. According to at least one account, Logan killed them both and escaped. Though pursued by Pinkerton detectives as well as other law enforcement officials, he made his way back to Montana. There, he decided to look up rancher James Winters, who was responsible for the death of his brother Johnny years earlier. He located Winters and killed him.

Logan returned to Knoxville. On November 30, 1902, he was playing pool when approached by several lawmen. Following a scuffle, Logan was subdued and arrested. He was tried for train robbery, found guilty, and sentenced to twenty years at hard labor. On June 27, 1903, Logan escaped. A rumor circulated that one of his guards had received a significant bribe to allow the prisoner to flee, but this was never proven. Logan fled to Colorado, where he made plans to rob another train. His target was a Denver and Rio Grande train, and the setting was near the small town of Parachute. As far as we know, it was to be Logan's last robbery, though the event and what became of Harvey "Kid Curry" Logan are shrouded in mystery.

CHAPTER 18

PARACHUTE, JUNE 7, 1904

Parachute seems like an unlikely name for this small Colorado town lying just north of the Colorado River in Fremont County. A nearby tributary is named Parachute Creek. According to one story, a member of the 1879 Hayden Survey observed that the watershed patterns of a nearby plateau north of town resembled parachute lines and thus chose the name for the area. Some argue that the arc of the ridgeline resembles the canopy of a parachute and that the several streams that flow toward the town remind one of the arrangement of the shroud lines. As early as 1910, however, it was written that the name "parachute" was a mispronunciation of a Ute Indian word, *pahchouc*, meaning "twins," and was the name used for a stream that ran between two nearly identical mountains found nearby.

The tracks for the Denver and Rio Grande Railroad ran through Parachute. During the early 1900s, Parachute was a center of fruit-growing activity, and the train would stop to load shipments. On June 7, 1904, the westbound train was halted three miles west of town by three men wearing masks. (At least one account claims five men.)

The robbery is layered with at least three compelling mysteries. For one, the details of the incident are murky, and to this day no one knows exactly what happened. For another, the robbery, according to some, marked the end of one of the most notorious train robbers of the era—Harvey "Kid Curry" Logan—but the truth remains elusive. And third, the dead man reputed to be Kid Curry may, or may not, have committed suicide.

When the Denver and Rio Grande run pulled into Parachute at 1:15 a.m. on the morning of June 7, a man stood waiting in the shadows, closely observing the activities of the crew. Following a brief inspection of the locomotive by the engineer and the loading of a small amount of freight, the train was preparing to pull away from the station when the man burst out of hiding, jumped into the locomotive cab, and pointed a revolver at engineer Ed Allison and fireman John Anderson. Convinced he had their attention, the stranger ordered the engineer to pull the train forward three miles and stop. At that point, at least two men, clearly accomplices of the first, appeared from the shadows.

After instructing the engineer and fireman to stand away from the locomotive, the outlaws made their way to the express car. (One account states it was the baggage car.) There, using threats, they forced the messenger to open the door. (Another account states that the door was dynamited.) According to one writer, the robbers were after a shipment of gold, believed to have been worth $150,000, but it has never been established that any gold was taken. Evidence suggests that the gold shipment in question was aboard an earlier train.

The outlaws applied a charge of dynamite to the express car safe, blew it open, and retrieved the contents, said to be cash. The railroad company never revealed the precise amount taken, at least not publicly. Following the robbery, the outlaws rode south across the Colorado River, heading for Battlement Mesa. Reportedly they were in no hurry and even stopped to steal horses along the way.

As soon as the outlaws galloped away, the engineer climbed back into the locomotive and returned the train to Parachute, where law enforcement authorities were notified of the robbery. Parachute lawmen were joined by others from Grand Junction, seventy miles to the southwest near the Utah border, as well as by some local ranchers. The posse from Grand Junction arrived by train in a short time, and soon all were hot on the trail of the robbers.

Fleeing the scene of the robbery, the outlaws crossed Battlement Mesa, then slowly made their way along Mamm Creek. To their surprise, the posse suddenly came into view on the trail several hundred yards behind them. For a few tense moments the two parties exchanged gunfire before the outlaws dashed away toward Divide Creek. There, they stole fresh horses from a rancher named Roll Gardner and continued eastward. A short time later, when Gardner discovered the missing horses, he grabbed his rifle, enlisted a neighbor, and set out in pursuit of the thieves. They soon overtook and rode along with the posse pursuing the robbers.

At East Divide Creek, the posse caught up with the outlaws once again. This time, the pursued thought it prudent to take shelter among some rocks. When the lawmen approached, the outlaws warned them away. The posse members responded by opening fire. Each of rancher Gardner's horses ridden by the train robbers was killed. At one point during the shooting, Gardner's neighbor ran from one place of concealment to another. As he did so, one of the outlaws rode up and was about to shoot him, when Gardner fired. His bullet struck the outlaw in the chest and knocked him to the ground. A few minutes later, the wounded man was heard yelling to his companions that he had been hit and was "going to finish the job." A moment later, a single shot rang out, followed by silence.

As the lawmen cautiously made their way toward the outlaws' hiding place, the two surviving bandits crept away on foot. The posse members came upon the dead man. He had a wound in his chest and one in his head. According to investigators, the head wound was self-inflicted. The money taken from the robbery was never found, and those who have researched this event believe the train robbers buried it somewhere along the trail as they fled.

The dead man was later identified as J. H. Ross, but it was soon learned that the name was an alias. The real J. H. Ross showed up at the sheriff's office and explained that he was not one of the bandits. Someone came forward and identified the corpse as Tap Duncan, a cowboy who worked on a nearby ranch. Later, at least two lawmen stepped forward and identified the dead man as Harvey "Kid Curry" Logan. Rowell Spence from the Pinkerton National Detective Agency, which pursued Kid Curry and a number of his fellow outlaws over the years, stepped forward and officially declared that the dead man was Logan. Noted western cowboy and lawman Charlie Siringo, working with the Pinkertons at the time, said the detective got it wrong, that it was not Curry. Enraged by the false identification, Siringo resigned from the agency. Special Agent A. W. Brown from the Denver and Rio Grande Railroad also came forth and stated positively that the dead man was not Kid Curry. Another railroad detective identified the corpse as that of George Bakerfield.

Whoever the dead man was, he was buried in the cemetery at Glenwood Springs, Colorado, under the name provided him by the Pinkertons. His grave lies a short distance from another noted western figure, Doc Holliday.

The two escaped train robbers were never identified. They may have been associated at one time or another with Butch Cassidy and the Hole-in-the-Wall Gang, but the truth was never learned.

Not long after the Parachute train robbery, rumors abounded that Kid Curry had not been the man killed. Even the Pinkertons, who initially identified the dead robber as Harvey Logan, kept a file containing information that he had escaped to South America and rejoined his old pals, Butch Cassidy and Harry Longabaugh, the Sundance Kid.

IDAHO

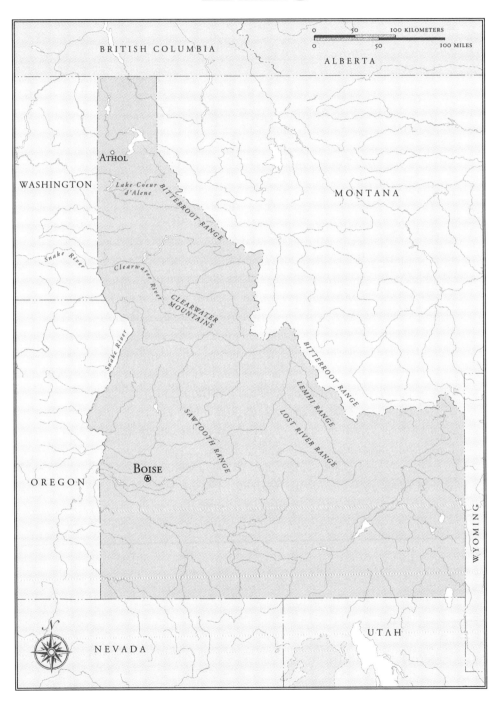

BRITISH COLUMBIA

ALBERTA

100 KILOMETERS

100 MILES

WASHINGTON

A°THOL

Lake Coeur d'Alene

BITTERROOT RANGE

MONTANA

Snake River

Clearwater River

CLEARWATER MOUNTAINS

Snake River

BITTERROOT RANGE

LEMHI RANGE

LOST RIVER RANGE

SAWTOOTH RANGE

BOISE

OREGON

WYOMING

N

NEVADA

UTAH

CHAPTER 19

ATHOL, SEPTEMBER 22, 1900

Athol is located in the lower part of Idaho's panhandle, twenty miles north of Coeur d'Alene. Some claim the town was named for the Scottish Duke of Atholl, but no one seems sure. From the early 1800s, Athol and the surrounding region attracted trappers and explorers, who established encampments on the nearby lakes and streams. The town amounted to little more than a trading post until 1882, when the Northern Pacific Railroad ran tracks through the area and constructed a station at Athol. By 1895, the town consisted mostly of railroad employees and homesteaders. Logging, milling, and agriculture soon followed.

On September 22, 1900, a most unusual event occurred: the Northern Pacific passenger train was robbed. The robbery was unusual, however, in that it was undertaken by a single individual. By this time, dozens of train robberies had occurred across the United States, but save for extremely rare instances, they were conducted by gangs of at least two or more. Rarely had a single train robber been successful until the Athol incident.

The train robber, whose identity remains a mystery to this day, boarded the train at Sandpoint, twenty-five miles northwest of Athol. Within an hour, the train pulled into Athol, where it unloaded passengers, mail, and freight and took on more. A half hour later, the Northern Pacific pulled away from the station.

Before it had gone one mile, a man described as five feet tall, slight of build, mustached, and wearing a dark suit and slouch hat rose up out of his seat in the first Pullman sleeper car. He had donned a mask and was brandishing a revolver.

He moved from berth to berth, quietly waking the sleeping passengers and, at gunpoint, ordered them to turn over their money and jewelry, which was placed in a canvas sack. None of the dazed passengers put up any resistance, and the stranger efficiently and effectively moved through the sleeper car. Before the sleepy travelers had gathered their wits and started dressing, the robber moved on to the second car, a passenger coach.

In a loud voice, the bandit announced that he wanted the riders to turn over their money and jewelry to him and to do it quickly. A moment later he walked through the Pullman carrying the sack into which the passengers tossed their valuables. According to an article in the *New York Times*, the robbery was "evidently carefully planned and was executed with a cool deliberation which showed the robber thoroughly understood his business." Most of the passengers were convinced that there was more than one robber. Finishing with the passenger coach, the robber moved on to the third car, a day coach. He had no sooner announced his intention to rob everyone than several women began screaming and attracting the attention of the conductor. The conductor entered the car and advanced toward the robber.

On spotting the conductor, who was carrying a revolver, the bandit turned and ran out of the car. At this point, the train was slowing down as it approached the station at Rathdrum, twelve miles southwest of Athol and near the Washington State border. The robber waited until the train pulled to a stop at the station, then jumped from the blind. Just as he landed on the station platform, the conductor fired two shots at him but missed. The robber raised his own revolver and hurriedly fired three shots back, one of which tore a piece of leather off one of the conductor's shoes. Carrying his canvas sack filled with money and jewelry, the robber turned and ran through the stunned crowd on the platform, into the station, and out another door.

Local law enforcement authorities were notified of the robbery, and a posse was formed. Witnesses stated that the robber fled on foot, heading south and out of town. The posse followed his tracks for three miles, to a point where they learned he had stolen a horse and raced away. Unable to follow, the posse returned to Athol.

The Athol train robber was never seen again and to this day has never been identified.

MONTANA

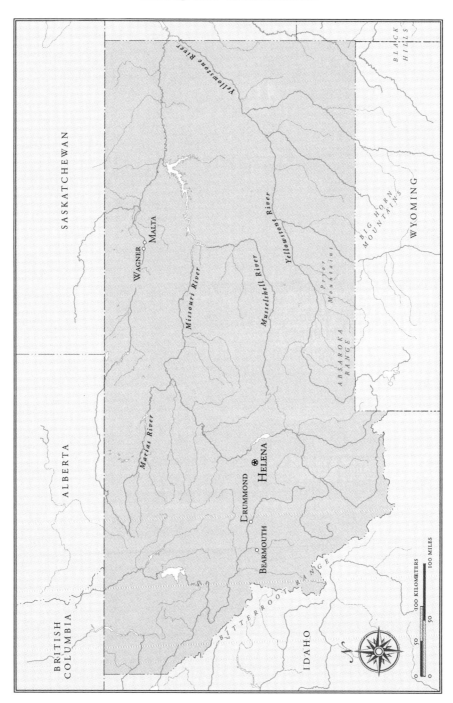

CHAPTER 20

THE SUNDANCE KID

The Sundance Kid, whose real name was Harry Alonzo Longabaugh, is inextricably linked to the better-known Butch Cassidy, most likely as a result of the 1969 western movie *Butch Cassidy and the Sundance Kid*, as well as subsequent print and film treatments. The two outlaws are often represented as boon companions participating in bank and train robberies together throughout their outlaw careers in both the United States and South America. Much of this is not true.

The Sundance Kid and Cassidy were indeed involved in a number of holdups and did in fact travel to South America together along with a woman, Etta Place. The truth is that the Sundance Kid was a relative latecomer in Cassidy's outlaw career. Most of the time, Cassidy's more or less constant companion was Elzy Lay.

Longabaugh was born near Phoenixville, Pennsylvania, in 1867, the last of five children of Josiah Longabaugh and Annie Place. Phoenixville is located a few miles northwest of Philadelphia. The original spelling of the family surname name was Langenbach.

Most accounts of Harry's youth portray him as unsettled and unstable. He was particularly close to his sister, Samanna. He often found refuge in reading books. When he was thirteen years old, Harry went to live with the Wilmer Ralston family in West

Harry Longabaugh, aka the Sundance Kid

Vincent, Pennsylvania, ten miles from Phoenixville. Though technically in the employ of Ralston, Harry was little more than an indentured servant. Shortly after turning fourteen, Harry left the Ralston household and drifted from one job to another.

During his travels, Harry discovered dime novels and purchased them whenever he had any spare change. He was particularly infatuated with the adventures and escapades associated with the desperadoes and outlaws of America's Wild West. Likely influenced by the novels, Harry purchased a revolver and taught himself to shoot. He eventually became quite skilled with the weapon.

When he was fifteen, Harry moved to Illinois to live with cousins. The cousins perceived greater opportunities for making a living in the West, so they sold the Illinois farm and moved to Durango, Colorado. Cousin George raised horses and employed Harry to break and train them. Two years later, they all moved to Cortez, Colorado. Harry continued to break horses for his cousin in addition to working on a neighboring ranch. In time, he grew to be a proficient horseman. During this time, Harry encountered men who would eventually play a major role in his life. They included Butch Cassidy, Matt Warner, Dan Parker, and others. In 1886, Harry traveled to Montana and secured a job on the N Bar N Ranch near Miles City. He was nineteen years old. There he met Wild Bunch member Harvey "Kid Curry" Logan.

Leaving his job at the N Bar N, Harry traveled to Wyoming in search of work. He arrived at the VVV Ranch near the town of Sundance. The winter of 1886–1887 was the worst in the history of the state of Wyoming. As a result, hundreds of head of cattle froze to death, and cowhands were laid off. With no prospects of a job and no money in his pockets, Harry stole a horse and saddle, a pair of chaps, and a revolver from two cowhands on February 27, 1887, and fled back to Miles City. Before he could effect a complete escape, the now twenty-year-old Longabaugh was overtaken and arrested by Crook County sheriff James Ryan on April 8. Locked in handcuffs and leg irons, Harry was placed aboard a train to be returned to Sundance. During the journey, he slipped out of his shackles and escaped by leaping from the moving train.

Oddly, Harry made his way back to Miles City. Along the way, he stole seven horses and sold them in the small town of Benton, Montana. In June, Deputy Sheriff E. K. Davis and stock inspector W. Smith located and arrested him. Once again shackled and chained, he was transported to the Sundance jail. In Sundance, he was tried for horse theft, found guilty, and sentenced to eighteen months at hard labor. While in jail, according to some writers,

Harry acquired the nickname by which he was known for the rest of his life: the Sundance Kid. Others have suggested that a fellow Wild Bunch companion bestowed the nickname on him after he was released from prison when he was twenty-two.

In search of work, Harry traveled to Deadwood, South Dakota, but had little luck in landing a job. Deadwood, a bustling mining town, was filled with saloons and gambling houses, and there, according to writers, Harry learned the finer points of card playing. There too he took up with some outlaws, which resulted in some troubles, one of which saw his friend Bob Minor shot dead by lawmen. Fearing for his own safety, Harry departed Deadwood, traveled to Cortez, Colorado, and returned to working with his cousin George breaking horses.

After several weeks of working on the ranch, Harry took up with Butch Cassidy, Matt Warner, and Tom McCarty. Though evidence is hard to come by, many believe that he was involved in the robbery of the San Miguel Valley Bank in Telluride, Colorado, with Butch Cassidy. On his own again, Harry returned to Montana and worked on ranches for a time. He also ventured into Alberta, Canada, where he broke and trained horses for the H2 Ranch near Fort Macleod. Some researchers are convinced he also found employment for a time with the Calgary and Edmonton Railway.

By autumn 1892, Harry had returned to Montana. Broke and with no work prospects, he decided to rob a train. Recruiting two men to assist him—Harry Bass and Bill Madden—Harry set his sights on the Great Northern No. 23 train, with the robbery to take place near the small Montana town of Malta.

CHAPTER 21

MALTA,
NOVEMBER 27, 1892

In 1892, Malta, Montana, was a somewhat remote and isolated stop for the Great Northern Railroad along its run from St. Paul, Minnesota, to Butte, Montana. It served primarily as a cattle-shipping depot. Malta, less than forty-five miles from the Canadian border, was granted its name during an application for a post office in 1890. When asked to come up with a name for what, at the time, was little more than a rail siding, one of the residents spun a globe, and when it stopped he closed his eyes and stabbed his finger at a location. It selected the island of Malta in the Mediterranean Sea.

Malta could be considered an ideal setting for a train robbery in 1892. It was far from any town of significant size, and its population so small that there was little need for lawmen. Perhaps this is why three men were intent on robbing the Great Northern Railroad No. 23 train at that station.

After dropping off a small amount of freight and mail at the small Malta station on November 27 (one account states that the robbery took place on September 29), the engineer signaled departure and a moment later pulled away. As the train was picking up speed, none of the town's few residents were about. Suddenly, three men ran out of hiding and jumped aboard the blind between the tender and the express car. They were later identified as Harry

Bass, Bill Madden, and Harry Longabaugh, the Sundance Kid. About a half mile from the station, the engineer was surprised when he heard a command from behind. He turned to find himself staring at a masked man who was pointing a revolver at him. Without wasting words, the intruder ordered the engineer to stop the train.

When the train finally pulled to a halt, the masked stranger instructed the engineer and fireman to climb out of the cab and lead the way back to the express car, where they united with the other two robbers. One of the bandits knocked on the door of the express car and told the messenger inside to open up. At first the messenger, Jerry Hauert, was inclined to resist, but the menacing tone of the outlaw discouraged him. A moment later he slid the door open, and the robber climbed inside, soon followed by the others. Once in the car, one of the outlaws told Hauert that they had no intention of harming him and that were only interested in any valuables that might reside within.

When they spotted the local safe, the robbers ordered Hauert to open it. When he did, the outlaws were discouraged to find only twenty dollars. (One report states that the bandits took two checks totaling $53.08 along with two packages valued at less than $11.) A moment later, they found the express safe and once again commanded Hauert to open it. The frightened messenger explained that he was unable to do so, that the safe could only be opened by express company agents stationed at St. Paul and Butte. They alone, said Hauert, knew the combination.

After rummaging through some of the packages in the express car and finding nothing of value, the robbers, discouraged by the small yield given their effort and risk, told the engineer and fireman to return to the locomotive. During the holdup, the masks of the outlaws kept falling away from their faces, and the messenger and engineer got good looks at them. Apparently deciding not to rob the passengers in the trailing coaches, the robbers jumped from the express car and ran off into the dark. The train proceeded to the next station, where the conductor telegraphed law enforcement authorities and explained the particulars of the robbery. The outlaws, as it turned out, returned to Malta.

Great Northern Railroad executive J. A. Mayer immediately offered a reward of $500 for the capture of each of the outlaws. The governor of Montana agreed to match that amount. The rewards amounted to considerably more than the robbers had stolen, but the railroad company was intent on sending a message that it would not tolerate train robbery.

Sheriff B. F. O'Neal of Choteau County organized and led a posse to search for the robbers. The group arrived in Malta on December 1 and decided to stop at the local tavern for a few drinks before setting out for the scene of the incident. In the same saloon were three strangers seated at a table near the back of the building: Harry Bass, Bill Madden, and Harry Alonzo Longabaugh. On spotting the lawmen, the three outlaws brought forth revolvers and rifles, threatened the posse members, and chased them away.

The train robbers decided it was time to leave town and began making preparations to do so. Unfortunately, they did not leave soon enough. Dogged railroad detective W. Ed Black located and arrested Bass and a companion named William Hunt a short time later. Around the same time, Sheriff O'Neal, along with Cascade County sheriff Joseph Hamilton, arrested Harry Longabaugh as he was boarding an eastbound train preparing to depart Malta. Madden could not be located.

Longabaugh and Bass, along with Hunt and another prisoner, were taken to Helena, where the conductor of the Great Northern No. 23 train identified them. Longabaugh gave his name as J. E. Ebaugh and stated that he sometimes used the alias J. E. Thibado. The prisoners were bound over for trial. Bail was set at $300 for each man, but neither of them had enough money. Two days later, Bill Madden was captured, arrested, and transported to Fort Benton, where he was placed in jail to await his trial. While in jail and under questioning, Madden admitted to his part in the train robbery and identified his partners as a man named Bass and another named "Loungbo."

The well-attended trial for the train robbers was held in Great Falls, Montana. The recommendation was made that "the prisoners be discharged for the reason that nothing has been adduced to show that they were guilty of the charge proffered against them." The case presented by the prosecution deteriorated, and the prisoners were released. As Bass was leaving the courthouse, he was immediately rearrested on charges of burglary based on statements made by Madden. Harry Longabaugh, the Sundance Kid, was allowed to leave town. Because he was using aliases, the prosecution was unaware that he was the "Loungbo" identified by Madden.

Bass and Madden were retried and convicted under the odd and rare charge of "burglary in the night time" in connection with the Malta train robbery. On Christmas morning 1892, both were admitted to the state penitentiary in Deer Lodge, Montana. Bass eventually received a pardon in January 1897 and, after leaving the prison, disappeared from the historical record. Madden was released in January 1898. He moved to Oregon City, Oregon, where he lived out the remainder of his life.

Harry Longabaugh was never rearrested and never faced trial for the Malta train robbery. A few weeks following his release, he found work on a ranch near Culberson, Montana. Among the ranch hands he worked with was Harvey "Kid Curry" Logan. In time, the two men became friends and served as members of the Wild Bunch, noted train robbers led by Butch Cassidy.

CHAPTER 22

BUTCH CASSIDY

The noted American outlaw known as Butch Cassidy was born Robert Leroy Parker on April 13, 1866, in Beaver, Utah, the first of thirteen children. (At least one account claims there were fourteen children.) Born into a loving and devoted Mormon family, he was raised to be loyal and honest.

Robert's father, Maximillian Parker, purchased 160 acres in Circle Valley, Utah, a broad flat plain surrounded by mountains. The fertile land, believed Parker, would be perfect for growing crops and raising cattle. Importantly, it looked like a fine place to raise a family. Parker moved his wife and six children into a two-room log cabin in 1879. Robert was thirteen years old.

During the first year on his new property, Maximillian Parker cleared the land, dug irrigation canals, and planted crops. His first harvest was successful. Over the next few years, Parker's cattle herd survived one of the coldest winters in Utah history. He also homesteaded additional property and added more land to his holdings. To make ends meet, Parker found work cutting mine timbers in a small mining town named Frisco. He also hauled wood for charcoal.

While Parker was working his own land as well as the additional jobs, squatters were becoming a growing problem in that part of Utah, and it was only a matter of time before he had to deal with them. Another family of Mormons had taken up residence

Butch Cassidy

on a portion of the new Parker homestead and was tilling the land and raising livestock. Because there existed little in the way of formal law enforcement in the area, and because Parker was committed to following the rules established by the Mormon Church, he reported the trespass to the local bishop and asked that the squatters be required to leave. In a surprising decision, the bishop judged the squatters more deserving of the land than Parker and awarded it to them. Parker had spent years, along with a great deal of money and energy, developing this property only to have church authorities take it away from him.

Having been treated unfairly, Parker had nothing to do with the Mormon Church thereafter. Young Robert Parker, after witnessing the unjust actions of the bishop, harbored contempt for the Mormon Church and disdain for religious hypocrites for the rest of his life. In time, he came to detest institutions that took advantage of those who could do little about it. These included not only the Mormon Church but also bank and railroad companies.

Robert Leroy Parker was only thirteen years old when he had his first encounter with the law. At the time he was working for a rancher named Pat Ryan not far from the town of Milford. The Parker family had debts to pay, and young Robert decided to contribute. He was described as dependable, intelligent, and capable of doing a man's work.

One payday, Robert rode into Milford to purchase a new pair of overalls. On arriving at the mercantile, he found it closed. Having already made the long journey into town and not wanting to wait around for the owner to return, he gained entrance, selected a pair of overalls, and left a note promising to return another day with payment.

Though Robert had the best of intentions, the owner of the mercantile deemed his action unacceptable and immediately reported it as a theft. Two days later, Robert was arrested. It was eventually determined that no crime had been committed, and he was released after two days.

The incident left several important impressions on young Robert Leroy Parker. First, he worried that the allegation of theft would embarrass his family, and he regretted any shame they might have to endure. Second, he was appalled by what he considered a bullying miscarriage of justice. From that point on, he harbored a certain contempt for the law.

At around the same time, Parker was arrested for stealing a saddle. It was never determined whether he was guilty of the charge, but while he was in jail the sheriff of Garfield County mistreated him badly. Angered by this, Parker, according to author

Charles Kelly, swore vengeance there and forevermore against lawmen.

Because he was brought up to be honest and forthcoming, Robert Parker presumed, in his youthful naïveté, that everyone else was too and that others would appreciate and understand such qualities in their fellow man. Young Robert's lack of worldly experience was in part responsible for this embryonic idealism. This was soon to change.

Robert left the Ryan ranch and went to work on the Marshall Ranch and Dairy around 1881 or 1882. The pay was better, and Robert received free milk, cheese, and butter, which he delivered to his family. According to area gossip, the Marshall Ranch served as a sometime headquarters for a gang of horse thieves and cattle rustlers. One member of this outlaw gang, a man named Mike Cassidy, had a reputation as a skilled breaker and trainer of horses. He was also an excellent shot with a handgun, said to have been able to put a bullet through a silver dollar at forty paces. The charismatic and likable Cassidy was idolized by the area's youth, who regarded him as a hero. Adults respected him, and he claimed a number of good friends.

Robert Leroy Parker was fascinated by Mike Cassidy from the first time they met at the Marshall Ranch. He was impressed with Cassidy's skills related to horses and cattle and taken with his disdain for the wealthy cattle barons. In time, Robert learned of Cassidy's outlaw activities. To him, it all sounded glamorous—a life filled with excitement and a certain level of danger as opposed to the tedium and hard work associated with his menial duties on the ranch.

Outlaw Mike Cassidy also grew fond of Parker and was impressed with the youth's hard work and skill with livestock. Cassidy spent a great deal of time with Robert, passing along his techniques for breaking and training horses. Cassidy gave Robert a saddle and instructed him in the finer points of horsemanship. In a short time, Robert was almost as skilled a rider as Cassidy.

Cassidy also presented Robert with a revolver, along with money to purchase ammunition. When they had time away from their ranch chores, Cassidy taught Robert how to handle the weapon. After weeks of practice, Robert was regarded as the best shot in the valley. Not long afterward, Cassidy ran afoul of the law and fled to Mexico, where, according to most reports, he remained until he died.

By the time Robert Parker was eighteen, he was five feet, nine inches tall and weighed 155 pounds. Though strong and durable, he remained soft-spoken and friendly to all. The year was 1884, and Robert informed his family that he was leaving the area, that he wanted to seek opportunities above and beyond those available in Utah. He said he was going to Telluride, Colorado, to seek work in the mines.

On arriving in Telluride, Robert, now calling himself Roy, secured a job loading ore onto pack mules and transporting it from the mines to the mills. When he received his paycheck, he always sent a portion of it home to his family.

Shortly after coming to Telluride, Parker sold his mare and arranged to keep an unbroken colt with a local rancher. Several months later, when he got some time off from his job, Parker decided to break the colt. He made several visits to the ranch, and each time the rancher offered to purchase the animal but was always turned down. One evening, when Parker went to the pasture, he took the colt to a different location to work with him. The rancher charged Parker with horse theft and requested that he be arrested. The rancher stated that the colt belonged to him and that he could produce several witnesses to testify to that effect.

Parker decided to leave the area but was arrested a short time later and placed in the county jail at Montrose. During a subsequent trial, Parker was found innocent of the charge. Shortly thereafter, he left Colorado for Wyoming. After working at a number of odd jobs, he traveled to Miles City, Montana. With few promising prospects, he decided to return to Colorado and made his way back to Telluride. While working at various tedious, ill-paying jobs, he met Matt Warner, another refugee from Utah and an ex-Mormon. The two became fast friends.

Warner earned his living racing horses. As Parker was a splendid horseman, the two teamed up. During a racing event in Cortez, Colorado, Parker made the acquaintance of Tom McCarty, Warner's brother-in-law. McCarty had a reputation as a horse thief, rustler, and gambler, and some believe he also robbed at least one bank. Some writers have also posited that McCarty and Warner were once members of Mike Cassidy's gang.

Most historical accounts have Robert Leroy Parker, aka Roy Parker, and Matt Warner robbing the San Miguel Valley Bank at Telluride. Some writers claim they were accompanied by Harry Longabaugh, known as the Sundance Kid, and Bert Madden, a sometime member of the notorious Wild Bunch. Additional research suggests that Dan Parker, brother to Robert, and a man named Bert Charter may have also taken part in the robbery. The robbers got away with $31,000. In no time at all, wanted posters were posted. Robert Parker was now officially an outlaw.

A short time later, according to some researchers, this same gang robbed a train, but evidence for such is scant. Parker, along with Warner and McCarty, traveled to Brown's Park (also known as Brown's Hole), located near a point where the borders of Colorado, Utah, and Wyoming come together. By the time the three had arrived at Brown's Park, Parker had decided to change his name. He now called himself Roy Cassidy, taking the surname of the man who had influenced him so greatly. A few weeks later, he changed his name again, this time to George Cassidy.

Eventually, George Cassidy found work on the Bassett Ranch, where he met and became friends with Elzy Lay. Cassidy and Lay had much in common: both were skilled horsemen and hard work-ers. In search of a better job with better pay, Cassidy made his way to Rock Springs, Wyoming, where he found work at Gottshe's Butcher Shop. In a very short time, the customers were calling him Butcher Cassidy, which was soon shortened to Butch. The nickname stuck, and from that point on Robert Leroy Parker was Butch Cassidy.

In time, Butch Cassidy found himself hanging out with the men who eventually became known as the Wild Bunch and the Hole-in-the-Wall Gang. They included Harry Longabaugh, Elzy Lay, Matt Warner, and others. All had run afoul of the establishment in one way or another. They planned bank and train robberies, not only for the money but also to thumb their noses at the railroad companies, the banks, and law enforcement, institutions that they believed preyed upon the working class. In particular, Butch Cassidy was eager to rob trains, and he soon found opportunities to do so.

CHAPTER 23

WAGNER, JULY 3, 1901

While history has long recorded this train robbery as taking place in Wagner, Montana, in truth it occurred at Exeter Switch, two miles east of the town. The robbery is notable for at least two reasons. First, one of the participants was Butch Cassidy, a colorful outlaw who went on to some level of prominence in large part as a result of novels and film. Second, it was the last train robbery perpetrated in Montana by the gang known for them: the Wild Bunch.

Wagner, located in northeastern Montana nine miles west of Malta, originally sat alongside the Northern Pacific Railroad line. Today Wagner is a small, unincorporated village on State Highway 2. Few people live there today.

Around midday on July 3, 1901, members of the Wild Bunch stopped and robbed the eastbound Great Northern Coast Flyer. It has never been entirely clear which members took part, but the available evidence suggests they included Butch Cassidy, Bill Carver, and either Ben Kilpatrick, Harvey "Kid Curry" Logan, or O. C. Hanks. According to witnesses, at least three men were involved, though some accounts provide for the possibility of more. Some writers insist Harry Longabaugh, the Sundance Kid, participated, but there is no evidence that he was involved.

During this time, the mastermind behind the Wagner train robbery was presumed to be Logan. Logan was familiar with the area, having worked on nearby ranches, and is believed to have had previous train robbery experience. Others have suggested that the idea to rob the Great Northern train came from Cassidy, who was fond of targeting major corporations like trains and banks because he thought they made their fortunes at the expense of the common man.

Though much has been written about this train robbery and its participants, the actual truth of what happened is unclear. For instance, confusion exists about how the train was actually halted. One account states that it was flagged to a stop near Exeter Switch and subsequently robbed. Another maintains that one of the outlaws (most believe it was Kilpatrick) either snuck aboard one of the coaches or jumped onto a blind, made his way across the tender, jumped down into the locomotive cab, and held the engineer at gunpoint. The argument has also been advanced that both the above occurred. Another account has Harvey Logan purchasing a train ticket and riding in one of the coaches before exiting and making his way toward the locomotive.

Once the train was stopped, the outlaws walked toward the express car, all the while firing their handguns at the passenger coaches to keep the occupants ducking for cover. Several were wounded by stray and ricocheting bullets. Once the express car was identified, the outlaws had it uncoupled from the rest of the train and ordered the engineer to pull forward two hundred yards.

The robbers broke into the express car with little difficulty but, once inside, encountered a locked safe to which the messenger was unable to provide access. A small charge of dynamite was applied but had no effect. Finally, after four attempts, the safe was opened and the contents withdrawn and placed in canvas bags carried by the robbers. Estimates of the amount taken have ranged from $40,000 to $83,000 in bank notes, a consignment headed to the Montana National Bank in Helena. Most researchers believe the smaller amount is the correct one.

As the robbery was taking place, one of the passengers climbed out of the car and began shouting at the outlaws and at one point fired a revolver at them. He was later determined to be a Montana sheriff. The robbers responded by returning fire with a volley and forcing the lawman back into the coach. On another occasion, one of the outlaws spotted someone leaning out of a passenger car window. Perceiving a threat, the outlaw raised his rifle and fired at the person. Unfortunately, he wounded an eighteen-year-old girl.

The bags of loot were carried to nearby horses and tied onto the backs of the saddles. The outlaws mounted up and rode across the nearby Milk River and continued south before turning east into what is today the Charles M. Russell National Wildlife Refuge. Lawmen who took up the chase conceded that the train robbers were "far better mounted than their pursuers, [had] already crossed the Missouri River, and [were] well on their way toward the 'Hole in the Wall' country in Wyoming."

Other lawmen argued that the robbers made their way to the "Bad Lands along the Missouri River, near the Little Rockies, and [were] there awaiting the time when the chase [had] grown cold." Eventually, the robbers, at least some of them, made their way to Miles City, where they spent some of the bank notes on fresh horses.

Not long after the robbery, the gang split up. A posse led by Sheriff Elijah Briant caught up with and killed Bill Carver. On December 12, 1901, Ben Kilpatrick was located and arrested in Knoxville, Tennessee; he was eventually tried and sent to prison. On December 13, Harvey Logan found himself involved in a shootout in Knoxville; he killed two policemen and escaped.

Butch Cassidy went on to great outlaw fame and was eventually glorified in books and movies. Years later reports were received that he and the Sundance Kid were killed in a shootout with Bolivian police. Subsequent investigations found this to be a fiction, and the prevailing evidence is that Cassidy returned to live out his life in the western United States under an assumed name (see *Butch Cassidy: Beyond the Grave* by W. C. Jameson).

CHAPTER 24

DRUMMOND, OCTOBER 23, 1902

The Northern Pacific train eastbound out of Missoula, Montana, on October 23, 1902, had departed the station there at 10:30 p.m. Engineer Dan O'Neill was in charge of the locomotive, which was pulling express, mail, and baggage cars as well as nine passenger coaches. O'Neill was on guard; in recent years, trains from the Northern Pacific as well as the Great Northern Pacific railroad companies had been robbed several times. O'Neill had heard reports that the Southern Pacific line had been held up over thirty times. Thus far, none of the trains worked by O'Neill and his fireman had been targeted. That was about to change.

As engineer O'Neill shepherded his train down the tracks around midnight, he spotted a waving red lantern in the distance ahead, the signal for caution. At this point, the Northern Pacific was two miles from its next stop at Drummond. Though he had his suspicions, the cautious O'Neill had little choice but to respond to the signal by slowing the train. When he turned toward his fireman to alert him to the impending stop, he spotted a stranger on the tender. Though it was dark, O'Neill thought the man was pointing a revolver at him.

O'Neill was unwilling to have his train robbed. One account states that instead of pulling to a stop, he opened the throttle and caused the train to speed up. O'Neill cannot be faulted for trying to save his train, but his decision not to stop cost him his life. Just as the train was picking up speed, the gunman on the tender fired. O'Neill dropped to the floor of the cab, dead.

A second version of the holdup has the robber stepping into the cab, telling O'Neill to do as instructed or be killed. The robber then turned to the fireman and ordered him to "go out and put that headlight out and be quick about it. And mind you, come back here." The fireman hastened to do as instructed, but before he returned to the locomotive, he heard a gunshot and saw O'Neill fall out of the cab and onto the ground, dead.

As the train proceeded down the tracks, the gunman told the fireman that he had robbed other trains, one in Oregon and two in Montana. The gunman shut off the steam and applied the brakes, bringing the train to a halt at Mulkey Canyon. At that point, the frightened fireman jumped from the cab and ran to the nearest cover in a grove of trees.

After the train had stopped, the robber walked back to the express car. As he approached, he noticed passengers looking out the windows of the coaches to see what was going on. He fired several shots in their direction, forcing them to take cover. On arriving at the express car, he pounded on the door and demanded that it be opened. When nothing happened, he threatened to blow the car up. At that, the two messengers inside slid the door open and came face to face with the robber, who pointed revolvers at them. He ordered both messengers out of the car, made them walk back up to the locomotive, and told them to uncouple the engine from the rest of the train. Unable to do so, the messengers were ordered back to the express car.

As the messengers watched, the robber applied a light charge of dynamite to the safe. When this charge had little effect, he then tied fifteen sticks of dynamite to it. The resulting explosion blew the express car to pieces but failed to open the safe. The robber then turned his attention to the registered mail pouches, forced the messengers to open them, and joked about his lack of success at robbing the train. He also expressed regret at having to kill the engineer. He explained that he was forced to do it because the engineer tried to resist.

When the robber had taken all he thought was of value, he jumped to the ground and ran toward the nearby trees. At least one account maintains that he had an accomplice, but that was never verified.

After the robber departed, the fireman managed to return the train to the station at Drummond. There, he had lawmen at Deer Lodge to the east informed of the robbery. A posse arrived by morning, inspected the scene, and followed a trail for two miles before losing it. The identity of the Drummond train robber remains a mystery to this day.

CHAPTER 25

BEARMOUTH, JUNE 16, 1904

The country to the east of Missoula, Montana, during the early 1900s was for the most part unpopulated, save for small trading posts and somewhat transient mining communities. One of these locations, about forty miles southeast of Missoula, was known as Bearmouth. Bearmouth had its origins in the mid-1800s as a trading post for the nearby mining communities of Beartown, Coloma, and Garnet. Today, Bearmouth is a ghost town. In 1904, however, it was the site of a major train robbery.

During the night of June 16, 1904, outlaws George Hammond and John Christie held up the Northern Pacific North Coast Limited 1.5 miles east of Bearmouth. Reports differ as to exactly how the robbery was initiated. One account states that Hammond and Christie, with revolvers drawn, approached the engineer and fireman while they were inspecting the locomotive at a regular water stop. A second report relates that the two train robbers jumped aboard the Northern Pacific as it was pulling away from the water stop. Whatever the truth, the outlaws escorted the engineer and fireman back to the express car.

It was never clear whether the express car messenger resisted any attempts by the robbers to enter. In fact, it is not clear if there was a messenger aboard this particular run at all. In any event, the express car door was blown open with a charge of dynamite. On

George Hammond

locating the safe inside the car, Hammond applied a charge to it. The explosion reportedly blew the safe forty feet into the air.

Likewise, it is unclear exactly what the robbers took from the safe. Initial reports stated that they stole $65,000, but much of the safe's contents were likely destroyed by the blast. A few days later, however, railroad company officials claimed that nothing of any value was missing.

After stuffing the take into canvas bags carried along for that purpose, Hammond and Christie turned and ran down the track in the direction from which the train had come. A passenger on the train named Annaweldt insisted that more than two robbers were involved. Annaweldt told investigators that after the robbers had departed, he followed them down the tracks for a short distance to a point where they veered off into the woods. He claimed to have heard Hammond and Christie talking with other men in the trees. Not wishing to be spotted, Annaweldt returned to the train. If there were, in fact, additional men, none played a role in the robbery other than to accompany or assist the perpetrators during their escape.

As soon as the Northern Pacific arrived at the closest station, a telegraph was sent to area law enforcement officials, and a posse was formed. With bloodhounds in tow, the posse arrived at the scene and almost immediately picked up the robbers' scent. With the dogs leading the way, the posse followed their trail for several miles, eventually arriving on the bank of the Hell Gate River. There they found evidence that the train robbers had transferred to a boat stashed nearby. Unused to pursuing escapees who took to flowing water, the posse gave up and returned.

A month went by with no progress on the case. Then, a woman with whom Hammond had become friendly informed police about his role in the train robbery and where he could be located. It turned out that Hammond bragged to the woman on several occasions about his escapade. Following up on leads, lawmen arrested George Hammond in Spokane, Washington.

During questioning, Hammond confessed to his part in the train robbery. He told the lawmen that, despite what the railroad company had stated, he and his partner had made off with about $3,500 and four hundred small diamonds. Hammond told authorities that he had cached a portion of train robbery loot near Coeur d'Alene, Idaho. With Hammond leading the way to the cache, lawmen recovered 350 diamonds and $225. Some believe that Hammond also participated in a train robbery in Oregon and another in Drummond, Montana, but this has never been proven.

During his interrogation, Hammond identified his partner as John Christie. A short time later, Christie was arrested. If additional men were involved in the robbery, as implied by the passenger Annaweldt, Hammond did not say. Hammond and Christie were tried, found guilty of train robbery, and sent to prison. Hammond, clearly the mastermind of the Bearmouth train robbery, was sentenced to fifteen years, Christie to seven.

NEVADA

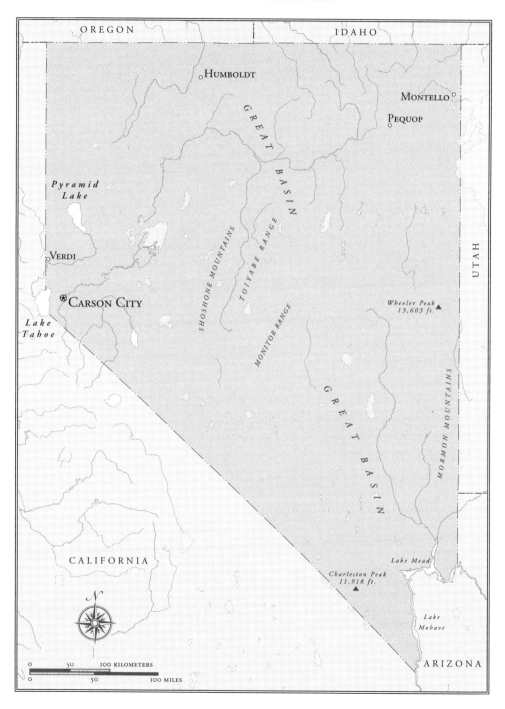

OREGON

IDAHO

HUMBOLDT

MONTELLO

PEQUOP

Pyramid
Lake

GREAT BASIN

VERDI

UTAH

SHOSHONE MOUNTAINS

TOIYABE RANGE

⊛ CARSON CITY

Wheeler Peak
13,603 ft. ▲

Lake
Tahoe

MONITOR RANGE

GREAT BASIN

MORMON MOUNTAINS

CALIFORNIA

Lake Mead

N

Charleston Peak
11,918 ft.
▲

Lake
Mohave

0   50   100 KILOMETERS

ARIZONA

0   50   100 MILES

CHAPTER 26

VERDI, NOVEMBER 4, 1870

The small town of Verdi, originally named O'Neill's Crossing for the man who built the bridge there, was renamed by Charles Crocker in 1868. Crocker was a founder of the Central Pacific Railroad and a fan of Guiseppe Verdi, the noted Italian opera composer. The town, which has a population of around fifteen hundred today, lies next to the state of California in southern Washoe County in the shadow of the Verdi Range and only a few miles from Reno.

Today Verdi is largely noted for its casinos and RV parks, but on November 4, 1870, it was the location of the first train robbery west of the Mississippi River.

It was a cold November night when the Central Pacific's No. 1 train pulled into the tiny Verdi station near the California border. It was 1:00 a.m., the train was running a bit behind schedule, and the conductor wanted to make the stop as brief as possible. In the express car, messenger Frank Marshall was napping. After leaving the Verdi station, the train would proceed eastward and arrive in Reno in less than an hour. There, Marshall would be responsible for handing over in excess of $40,000 in gold and silver coins to the manager of the Wells, Fargo office.

At the Verdi station, five men waited for the train. To anyone who happened to glance their way, they would look like passengers waiting for their coach to arrive. In truth, the five had other plans: they intended to rob the express car and make off with the fortune in coins. In the distance, the train whistle could be heard, and a moment later the engine's headlight could be seen piercing the darkness. When the train pulled to a stop, the doors to the coaches opened to let a handful of passengers out. Two of the men standing on the platform moved over to the coal tender behind the locomotive and, unseen, scrambled to the top. The other three remained where they were.

As the conductor, D. G. Marshall (unrelated to the messenger), prepared for the train's departure, he noticed the three men standing on the platform. He assumed they were waiting to board the train but had missed the call. Marshall stepped out of the coach and approached the three to collect their fares. Much to his surprise, the men pulled out their revolvers and pointed them at the conductor. Marshall was forced back into the coach, made to sit in one of the seats, and told to ensure the passengers remained where they were. Moments after the conductor had received his instruction from the outlaws, the train began to pull away from the station.

Marshall was indignant at the treatment he received. As soon as the three outlaws turned their attention to the passengers, Marshall, realizing the train was going to be robbed, stood and yanked the bell cord to signal the engineer to halt the train, only to discover that it had been cut. Up at the head of the train, the two outlaws stationed atop the coal tender dropped down into the locomotive cab and, at gunpoint, ordered the engineer to stop the train. As he was trying to decide his next move, Marshall noticed that the train was starting to slow down.

As soon as the train stopped, Marshall watched as the three gunmen jumped from the coach to the ground and made their way toward the locomotive. Marshall cautioned the passengers to remain seated and calm. He went to his service box and searched for something to use as a weapon. All he could find was a hand axe. Though the tool was insufficient to combat the guns of five outlaws, the determined Marshall hefted it, then climbed out of the coach and moved toward the locomotive.

While conductor Marshall was searching for a weapon, the outlaws forced the engineer back to the express car and instructed him to uncouple it. Marching him back into the locomotive, they then ordered him to pull forward. Before conductor Marshall could reach the express car, it was moving down the track. The rest of the train, now without an engine, rested on a moderately steep downgrade. With nothing to stop it, the train could begin rolling downhill, picking up momentum, and possibly crash into the express car ahead. Concerned for the safety of the passengers, Marshall was about to instruct the brakeman to set the brakes when he heard two sharp blasts from the engine, a signal from the engineer to do just that. Moments later, the engine, tender, and express car, now out of sight and hearing, pulled to a stop near an abandoned stone quarry six miles east of Verdi.

By this time, express car messenger Marshall had deduced that a robbery was in progress. Though equipped with at least one firearm to be used to defend the contents of the car, Marshall was nervous and unsure about being caught in a gun battle. Minutes passed, and he could hear men approaching the express car, their boots crunching on the railroad gravel as they walked. When they rapped on the car door and demanded that he open it, Marshall wasted no time. He slid open the heavy wooden door and looked out at several men in masks pointing handguns at him.

The robbers ordered the engineer and fireman into the express car and, along with messenger Marshall, marched them into a small room in the back where the mail was kept. They were pushed inside and the door closed and bolted behind them. After forcing conductor Marshall to lead them to the safe, one of the robbers took little time in picking the lock. The contents—gold and silver coins—were placed into canvas bags. When the safe had been emptied, the robbers jumped from the express car, ran to horses picketed nearby, and rode away. In all, according to Wells, Fargo reports, a total of $41,600 in twenty-dollar gold pieces and $8,000 worth of silver ingots was taken, although the Central Pacific reported the amount as $150,000. Wells, Fargo and Company offered a reward of $10,000 for the recovery of any or all of the stolen cargo and the arrest of the robbers.

On being notified of the Verdi train robbery, Wells, Fargo officials immediately assigned F. T. Burke to investigate and, hopefully, identify and capture the robbers. Burke had been employed by Wells, Fargo for years and possessed impeccable credentials as a detective and man hunter. Up until the Verdi train robbery, Burke's assignments had mostly been associated with stagecoach holdups. His most effective technique for identifying robbery suspects was to insert as many agents as possible into an area and have them hang out with locals, listening to conversation and gossip about who might have suddenly come into some money. Burke decided the best, and closest, place to undertake this process was in the nearby town of Reno.

While Burke and his men were circulating throughout Reno, Sheriff Charley Pegg, along with his undersheriff, James H. Kinkead, and other lawmen, followed the trail the outlaws took when escaping into the nearby mountains. The robbers stopped at an abandoned quarry, where they made a brief camp before moving on. It was soon discovered that all the telegraph wires west of Reno had been cut. Western Union officials were alerted, and the wires were repaired by the following morning.

Within a week, Burke's agents identified a local resident known to be out of work but who appeared to have come into possession of a significant amount of cash. No sooner had he been arrested and set for questioning than another man, also out of work but spending freely, was also taken in. In a short time, a third man was also apprehended. All three of the men, according to Burke, were well acquainted with one another.

One of those arrested was a sometime carpenter named R. A. Jones. Under questioning, Jones caved, confessed to his role in the train robbery, and identified the two other detainees, James Gilchrist and John Davis, as well as two others, Tilton Cockerill and John Squiers, as his partners in the crime. He also identified the man who had planned the robbery and recruited the others to conduct it. He was John T. Chapman, a former Sunday school teacher. Cockerill, Davis, Gilchrist, and Squiers had previous records. The robbery was Jones's and Chapman's first venture into crime. All the men involved in the robbery had been rounded up and arrested within four days of the incident.

Lawmen regarded John Davis as the worst of the bunch. He had been a mineworker but was unsatisfied with his wages. He decided the quickest and easiest way to make a lot of money was to rob stagecoaches. From numerous stagecoach robberies, he acquired a quantity of gold and silver bullion. Because most of the ingots were inscribed with company names and identification marks, Davis constructed a small smelter where he melted down the bars and recast them. So proficient was he in this endeavor that he went into business and opened a small mill and smelter in nearby Six Mile Canyon. At one point he was apprehended for possessing stolen bullion but was acquitted. The rumor in Reno was that Davis had bribed several members of the jury.

Like Davis, John Chapman longed for a higher standard of living and believed he could gain one by stealing the shipment from the express car. Chapman traveled to San Francisco, where he visited the offices of the Central Pacific Railroad Company as well as Wells, Fargo. Thus, he learned that a large shipment of gold and silver coins was being readied for transport via express car. When he had all the information he needed about the railroad schedules and cargo, he telegraphed Davis and his companions, who readied themselves for the heist.

Before long, every one of the robbers was under arrest, but only $7,000 of the stolen shipment was recovered. Each man, save for Jones and Gilchrist, insisted on his innocence. Gilchrist eventually led Wells, Fargo authorities to another $30,000 worth of the stolen shipment.

The Verdi train robbers were tried, convicted, and sentenced to prison terms ranging from five to twenty-three years. Jones got five years. Chapman and Squiers each received twenty-three. All of them served their entire sentences, save for John Davis. After spending five years in the Nevada State Penitentiary, Davis found himself in the midst of a prison break in which several guards were killed, others were wounded, and the warden was held prisoner. The prisoners had taken control of the facility. Instead of joining the reveling inmates, Davis rendered aid to the wounded officers. For this he was pardoned shortly thereafter.

Within a year of his release, Davis was killed while attempting a stagecoach robbery in White Pine County, Nevada. Eugene Blair, the shotgun rider, blew out Davis's chest with a load of buckshot.

The rest of the Verdi train robbers served out their sentences and were never heard from again, except for John Squiers. After walking out of prison, Squiers traveled to California, where he got into trouble and was convicted of trying to bribe a jury. He was sent back to prison. This time he got five years at California's San Quentin.

According to records, of the gold and silver taken in the Verdi train robbery, most was recovered. A total of 150 twenty-dollar gold pieces remained missing. Since the bandits did not have enough time to spend that much money, they presumably buried it somewhere near the robbery scene, along the escape trail, or near the stone quarry where they made camp. To this day, people continue to search for the missing coins, which have been assessed a collector's value of around $500,000.

CHAPTER 27

PEQUOP, NOVEMBER 5, 1870

Pequop, Nevada, is today a ghost town in the northeastern part of the state not far from the larger town of Wells. The tiny community had little to claim as noteworthy and remained indistinct and unknown save for one thing: it was the site of the second train robbery in the United States west of the Mississippi River. Some accounts refer to this event as the Independence train robbery. At the time, Independence was a slightly larger town located several miles to the west of Pequop. The first train robbery in the western United States, interestingly, had occurred only twelve hours earlier at Verdi, Nevada. Both robberies targeted the same express car. The express messenger, Frank Marshall, was assigned to both runs of the Central Pacific train.

Express messenger Frank Marshall (one account gives his name as Frank Minch) had learned from the train robbery at Verdi hours earlier to hide the money before the robbers could enter the car. On this November 5 eastbound Central Pacific passenger run, the express car was transporting $20,000 in cash and gold coins.

When the train arrived at Pequop, a gang of five robbers forced the engineer to detach the express and mail cars from the rest of the train and pull several hundred yards ahead. As this was transpiring, messenger Marshall took most of the money and gold from the safe, carried it to the far end of the car, and hid it among boxes and bags of freight. He left $3,000 in the safe. He then blew out the lantern and awaited the robbers' approach.

When the outlaws pounded on the express car door and demanded that it be opened, Marshall acquiesced. After climbing in and locating the safe, they ordered Marshall to open it. He did so willingly. Marshall even reached into the safe and pulled out the $3,000 he had left in there. Delighted with the take, as well as the fact that the robbery had gone so smoothly, the outlaws rode away. The next day, Wells, Fargo offered a reward of $2,500 for the capture of the robbers and another $2,500 for the return of the stolen money. At first, law enforcement authorities believed that the robbers of the Central Pacific near Pequop might be the same as those who conducted the robbery a few hours earlier at Verdi, but they soon realized that two different gangs were involved.

Unfortunately for the outlaws, one of them had dropped some items on the floor of the express car during the robbery: a glove and a brass compass. The glove had the name "Edward Carr" inked onto it, and the compass was engraved with the name "William Harvey." After the robbery was reported and the evidence submitted, it was quickly learned that Carr and Harvey were deserters from the Third US Cavalry stationed at Camp Halleck.

Edward Carr had fled from the army post after being identified as a suspect in the murder of a woman. He had been spending time and money in a house of prostitution located two miles south of the camp and owned by a woman named Sallie Whitmore. Carr got involved in a heated discussion with an army sergeant that erupted into a fight. Angered, Carr rode back to the camp, retrieved his rifle, and raced back to Sallie's. He shot at the sergeant but missed and struck Whitmore, killing her. Carr was arrested and incarcerated at Camp Halleck. Before he could be transferred to Elko for trial, Carr, along with five other soldiers, deserted. Both Carr and Harvey immediately became suspects in the Pequop train robbery. As it turned out, neither was involved in the heist.

Days later, a posse caught up with four men not far from the Deep Creek station on the Overland Telegraph Road. Two escaped, but Leander Morton and Daniel Baker were arrested. Morton was wearing a pair of buckskin gloves inscribed in ink with the name "W. H. Harvey." The evidence connected the two men with the train robbery, but neither was a deserter from the army. How Morton came into possession of Harvey's gloves was never learned.

A few days later a third man, Daniel Taylor, was arrested. Not long after, a fourth suspect, George Lee, was captured but escaped the next day. He was never found. The fifth robber was never identified.

Taylor, Baker, and Morton were charged with robbing the Wells, Fargo express car as well as stealing US mail. The other members of the gang were never found. The deserters Carr and Harvey, along with their companions, were likewise never found, and some researchers believe that Taylor, Baker, Morton, and other gang members killed them.

In late November, Baker, Morton, and Taylor confessed to their role in the robbery of the Central Pacific train at Pequop. In January 1871, the three went on trial at Elko. On January 15, the jury deliberated only a few minutes before arriving at a verdict. Although train robbery was a hanging offense, the criminals were each given thirty-year sentences in the Nevada State Penitentiary at Carson City. They were delivered to the prison on January 19.

They had not been incarcerated for long when they helped organize an escape. Baker and Morton, along with twenty-seven other "desperate outlaws," broke out of the prison and fled into the nearby countryside. Along the way they stole clothing and murdered at least two men. Morton and a man named Black were overtaken by a posse made up of area farmers and led by a Paiute Indian tracker. During the ensuing confrontation, Black killed the Indian, and the two escapees grabbed two horses and fled.

Two days later the same posse caught up with Morton and Black in the sand hills southeast of Round Valley. Morton surrendered. When Black raised his hands, he was shot in the head by another Indian tracker. The Indian claimed he thought Black was raising a weapon, but some believe he was shot in retaliation for killing the tracker two days earlier. The two escapees were taken to the nearest town, where Black died from his wound.

As two of the farmers dug a grave for Black, the rest took Morton to a nearby tree and hanged him. His body was tossed atop Black's and the grave refilled. Lawmen arrived the next day and queried the farmers as to what had transpired. The farmers simply explained that the two men had died. They refused to tell the lawmen where to find the bodies.

Daniel Baker managed to elude his pursuers, eventually fleeing to Corvallis, Oregon. In 1874, Wells, Fargo detectives located him there and arrested him. Baker was married, employed, and regarded as an honest, respectable citizen. He was returned to Carson City, where he served two years before being pardoned on January 15, 1878.

CHAPTER 28

MONTELLO, JANUARY 23, 1883

In the annals of American train robbery, the historical record shows that the bandits were successful a great percentage of the time. On rare occasions, a brakeman, conductor, or engineer played a role in thwarting a robbery, but for the most part these employees remained passive to avoid being killed or injured. On even rarer occasions, an express car messenger emerged as a force responsible for foiling a train robbery. One example is Aaron Yerkes (sometimes spelled Yerx) Ross, a messenger in charge of the contents of a Wells, Fargo express car on an eastbound Central Pacific train that stopped at the railway station in Montello, Nevada, on January 23, 1883.

In 1883, Montello, located in northeastern Nevada, ten miles from the Utah border, was little more than a brief stop for the east- and westbound Central Pacific trains. At the time it consisted of the train station, a water tank, a shed for wood harvested for fuel, a tool shed, and a couple of crude shacks. Twenty years later Central Pacific became Southern Pacific, and due to increased traffic and a need for greater support systems, Montello grew slightly. Today, the population is less than ninety. The name Montello was assigned to the location in 1912. Before that, it was known as Bauvard. Montello is believed to be a Shoshone Indian word for "rest."

It was 1:00 a.m. on January 23 when the Central Pacific train pulled into the Montello station. Express car messenger Ross had been sleeping and came awake when the train stopped. Groggy from his slumber, he readied himself in the event that he was needed to perform any duties. Unbeknownst to him, Montello was not a scheduled stop on this run. Moments earlier, the engineer spotted a signal that indicated a need to pull in at the station. Little did he know that it was the initiation of a robbery attempt.

After the train came to a stop, an undetermined number of armed men approached the locomotive and ordered the engineer and fireman to remain where they were and not interfere. Various reports estimated the gang of robbers ranged from five to a dozen or more. While two of the robbers remained to guard the railroad employees, the rest walked down the station platform to the express car. They pounded on the door and demanded that the messenger open up. By this time, Ross was fully awake and aware of what was transpiring. He made a decision that was to change his life.

Aaron Ross was no stranger to holdups and bandits. In the not too distant past he had been a stagecoach driver in Montana. On two occasions robbers had stopped the Concord stage he was driving. Ross, fifty-three years of age, six feet, four inches tall, 250 pounds, and aggressive in demeanor, was no shrinking violet. On the first attempted heist, he hesitated not one second as he pulled out a shotgun and attacked the bandits. Unaccustomed to this kind of response, the outlaws hurried away. During the second robbery attempt, a forceful defense of the coach by Ross forced the bandits to leave one of their companions lying dead in the road.

When Ross heard the train robbers outside the express car demanding that he open up, he responded by arming himself with his revolver. Stalling for time, Ross opened the express car door slightly, looked out at the bandits, and said that he needed a couple of minutes to get his boots on. Later he said he estimated there were five or six men. The robbers told him to "hop out" and put his boots on later. Ross responded by slamming the car door and locking it. The robbers resumed pounding on the door. Assessing the odds, Ross walked over to a rack on the side of the car and removed a Winchester rifle. As far as he knew, he was the only armed employee on the train.

All of a sudden, the train lurched forward and proceeded down the track. From a distance, Ross heard the whistle of the westbound No. 2 train and realized that the eastbound he was on had been shunted onto a siding to prevent a collision. When the train came to a halt, the outlaws, according to Ross, "stationed one man at each corner of the [express] car and started shooting with their rifles." The volley of shots crisscrossed through the express car. One of the bullets wounded Ross in the hand, nearly taking off a finger. Another bullet struck him in a hip, and yet another passed through flesh just below his ribs. Ross sought shelter behind an iron safe and some furniture. From his position, Ross fired back through the walls of the car, aiming toward the sounds of the guns.

A shot from one of the outlaws destroyed the express car lamp hanging from the ceiling. In pitch blackness, Ross, despite his damaged finger and bleeding badly from his wounds, reloaded the rifle and fired back several rounds through the wooden sides of the car. The floor was becoming slippery with his blood. One of the robbers had climbed atop the express car, apparently in search of an opening. Ross listened to the outlaw's footsteps and, when he was certain he had pinpointed his location, fired a shot through the roof. He heard the man drop from the top of the car to the station platform.

From inside the car, Ross heard the westbound Central Pacific train slowing down. Just before pulling to a stop next to the eastbound locomotive, the engineer leaned out of his cab to ask what was wrong. Instead of the eastbound engineer, one of the outlaws stuck his head out of the cab and ordered the westbound engineer to keep moving down the line. As the westbound train proceeded up the track, the conductor peered out one of the coach windows and saw what he estimated to be eight to twelve outlaws wearing masks and carrying rifles. The westbound train picked up speed and moved on.

As Ross lay bleeding in the cold express car, he assumed the westbound engineer would stop at the next station and telegraph the Montello situation to law enforcement authorities. He wondered how long it would take for help to arrive.

In the meantime, from noises he heard outside, Ross deduced that the robbers had uncoupled the mail car from the front of the express car. He listened intently as the locomotive pulled away, taking the tender and mail car farther up the track. Ross heard the train stop and then begin to back up rapidly. It dawned on him what was happening: the outlaws had decided to crash the mail car into the express car, hoping their target car would telescope and split, enabling them to enter. Ross braced himself for the impact.

When the backward moving train collided with the express car, nothing happened as the outlaws had planned. The express car was constructed of heavier steel, and its frame was stout and strong. The impact, however, caused both doors of the express car to spring open. When the robbers saw this, they ran toward the car, expecting to gain entrance. They had not reckoned on the determined Aaron Ross.

Ross jumped up from behind his barricade and slammed both doors shut before the outlaws could climb in. Having failed to lock them, Ross was surprised when one of the doors suddenly slammed open again. On his knees and still bleeding from his wounds, he watched as one of the robbers attempted to climb through the opening, rifle in hand. In the darkness of the interior of the express car, the outlaw did not see Ross rise from his position and approach. When a few feet from the intruder, Ross kicked him with a heavily booted foot, knocking him out of the car and onto the ground. Outlaws and railroad employees could hear Ross's laughter from several yards away.

The outlaws then made a halfhearted attempt to set fire to the car, but this failed because they did not give the feeble blaze enough fuel, and it quickly burned out. Growing frustrated, the outlaws fired their weapons into the express car once again in a final barrage. When they paused to reload, they could hear an approaching locomotive coming to the rescue. Deciding they had had enough, they turned and raced toward their horses. Peering out through one of the many bullet holes, Ross was certain he saw five men in retreat. One of them, he noted with satisfaction, was bent over as if from a severe bullet wound. It was later learned that Ross had killed one of the bandits and wounded at least three others.

Had the robbers managed to enter the express car and broken into the safe, they would have retrieved only around $600 for their troubles. The mail car, which had been destroyed in the collision, had been transporting more than $250,000 guarded by three unarmed and inexperienced mail clerks.

Two posses were formed and set out in pursuit of the outlaws. One was led by Sheriff William Brown of Ogden, Utah, and the other by Sheriff Turner of Utah County, Utah. Four of the robbers were captured south of the Great Salt Lake and returned to Nevada. They were tried, found guilty, and sentenced to the Nevada State Penitentiary for terms ranging from twenty to forty years.

None of Ross's wounds were serious, and he recovered with no difficulty. Wells, Fargo and Company heralded him as a hero. He was provided transportation to company headquarters in San Francisco, where he was feted and given a certificate proclaiming his bravery and loyalty to the company, a gold watch valued at $650, and a monetary award of $1,000. In his later years, Ross was assigned to guard large shipments of gold and silver bullion. He retired from Wells, Fargo and lived out the remainder of his life in Ogden, Utah.

CHAPTER 29

HUMBOLDT, JULY 14, 1898

Once outlaws or outlaw gangs gain a reputation as effective and efficient perpetrators of crime, along with accompanying press releases, they become fixed in the minds of both the public and law enforcement officers. For example, researchers point out that more bank and train robberies, as well as other criminal acts, have been attributed to Jesse James than he was ever involved in. If a train got robbed during his era, most assumed that James and his gang were responsible.

The same holds true for another noted train robbery gang: the Wild Bunch. This band of successful outlaws included, at various times, noted train robbers such as Butch Cassidy, Harry "The Sundance Kid" Longabaugh, Harvey "Kid Curry" Logan, Elzy Lay, George "Flat Nose" Curry, and others.

Unsurprisingly then, when a Southern Pacific train was held up near Humboldt, Nevada, and upward of $26,000 was stolen, the heist was attributed to the Wild Bunch. In this case, though precise details are hard to come by and many are contradictory, a number of writers have focused on the notion that the actual robbers included Wild Bunch members the Sundance Kid, Kid Curry, and Flat Nose Curry.

Humboldt is located in northern Nevada's Humboldt Range. In 1860, a French trader named Louis Barbeau discovered silver in the area, and soon a rush was on, even though it was Paiute

Indian country and regarded by many as hostile territory. What was originally called Humboldt City was platted in 1861, and by 1863 the population was recorded at five hundred. Two hundred houses were constructed, along with hotels, saloons, a blacksmith's forge, and two mercantiles. Businessmen were hopeful that the city would grow, but by 1864 ore production had declined to the point where Humboldt could no longer be supported. Today it is a ghost town, and the ruins of the 150-year-old town can still be seen.

At 1:25 a.m. on July 14, 1898, two strangers climbed into the engine cab of the eastbound Southern Pacific train as it idled at Humboldt Station, preparing for departure. At gunpoint, they instructed the engineer to pull one mile ahead, where a third outlaw awaited on horseback, leading two saddled but rider-less mounts. The engineer was instructed to stop the train near the rider. After ordering the engineer to exit the cab and lie down on the ground, the outlaws withdrew several bundles of dynamite from the saddlebags on their horses.

After striding over to the express car with the explosives, the bandits called for the express messenger, a man named Hughes, to open the door. Curious passengers leaned out the windows of the coaches, observing the goings-on. They were spotted by one of the outlaws, who fired several rounds in their direction, forcing them to take cover inside.

When messenger Hughes refused to open the express car door, the outlaws, with no further comment, attached a bundle of dynamite to it and blew it apart. Climbing into the car and over the stunned messenger, the robbers located the safe, attached another, large charge of dynamite to it, and lit the fuse. The outlaws then scrambled out of the car to safety, taking the messenger with them.

The resulting blast destroyed much of the express car. After locating the wrecked safe among the debris, the outlaws stuffed the contents into canvas bags brought along for that purpose. Estimates of the take ranged from $450 to $26,000, along with some jewelry.

Reports were made, and posses soon arrived at the scene of the holdup and located the robbers' tracks. With the information that the robbers fled toward the north, perhaps heading for Idaho, the lawmen made a halfhearted attempt to follow but apparently had deficient tracking skills. In addition, a lack of preparation found them without adequate supplies and provisions. With little provocation, they abandoned the pursuit. Several days later, law officers arrested four men and charged them with the robbery. The four, who had nothing to do with the holdup, were eventually acquitted.

The principal advocate for the notion that Flat Nose Curry, Kid Curry, and the Sundance Kid robbed the Southern Pacific train at Humboldt is writer Donna Ernst, who claims to be a descendant of the noted and colorful Harry Longabaugh. The truth of who was responsible for the robbery may never be known, but thus far Ernst presents the most compelling argument that it was members of the Wild Bunch.

NEW MEXICO

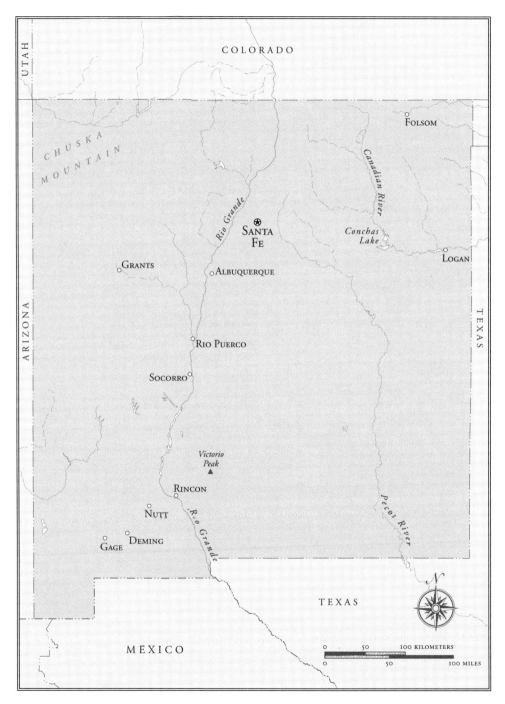

CHAPTER 30

RINCON, APRIL 16, 1882

The Rio Grande, known by most as the great river that functions as the border between the United States and Mexico, also bisects the state of New Mexico on its journey from north to south. Here and there, extensive and fertile flood plains enable significant agriculture. In the southern part of New Mexico, the small town of Rincon (Spanish for "corner") lies in a region largely given over to the growing of chilis. Today, the town's population is less than three hundred. In 1882, Rincon was little more than a watering and fuel stop for the Santa Fe Railroad. Train robbery was unknown to the residents and railroad employees in the village, but that was about to change.

In April 1882, rumors circulated throughout that part of New Mexico that an eastbound Santa Fe train would be transporting $200,000 in silver ingots bound for a bank in New York. The silver was a product of the nearby mines. On learning of the shipment, a group of five men decided to stop the train and take the silver.

April 16 was a Sunday, and the Santa Fe train made its way toward the Rincon station well past sundown. A few miles out of town and far from habitations, the masked and heavily armed train robbers had piled large rocks onto the tracks to stop the train. Unlike most train robbers who resorted to track obstructions, these men did not wave a red lantern to warn the engineer of an imminent obstacle. As the train rumbled toward the obstruction, the outlaws took up a position some distance away from the impending wreck. The locomotive slammed into the rock pile and was immediately derailed, followed by the tender, the express car, and the baggage car. The engineer and fireman were killed instantly, and the express car messenger was badly injured.

Once the dust had settled, the bandits rushed forward to what they thought was the express car but was in reality the baggage car. They had a difficult time opening the door of the wrecked car but managed after several minutes. Once inside, however, they grew confused when they could not locate a safe or anything containing the silver they expected to find. While the outlaws were rummaging around in the baggage car, the conductor, along with a number of armed passengers, quickly organized into a force intending to drive away the robbers. Led by the conductor, they made their way from the passenger cars toward the baggage car, handguns at the ready.

The train robbers spotted the oncoming conductor and passengers. Frustrated by not finding the silver and now panicked by the show of force, the outnumbered bandits decided to give up the attempt and flee. Leaping from the damaged baggage car, they ran to their horses and rode away. The robbery of the Santa Fe train was thwarted but still exacted a great cost in human life and damage to the train.

When notified of the attempted robbery and the wrecked train, law enforcement authorities formed a posse. At the scene, however, the lawmen failed to locate the trail of the bandits. Suspicions were voiced, and names of suspects were exchanged. Most believed a gang of robbers who had plagued New Mexico and eastern Arizona during the previous year was responsible, but nothing was ever proven.

CHAPTER 31

GAGE, NOVEMBER 24, 1883

O ver the years bandits came up with a number of different ways to stop massive trains long enough to complete their robberies. They piled obstructions such as rocks and boulders, trees, and railroad ties upon the tracks, stationed themselves well ahead of the locomotive and swung a red lantern to signal the train to slow or stop, inserted themselves into the cab of the locomotive, and forced the engineer to pull to a halt. One of the most effective ways to stop a train—removal of one of the rails—was employed at a location near Gage Station, New Mexico, on November 24, 1883.

Gage Station was a small siding along the Southern Pacific Railroad line running east-west in southern New Mexico. The official name of the town was Gage; railroaders always knew it as Gage Station. Gage served as a center for ranching and railroad activity in this somewhat remote part of New Mexico until around 1930, at which time it had an estimated population of one hundred. Since then, it has achieved the status of a ghost town, and today little of it remains.

At around 5:00 p.m. on November 24, 1883, Southern Pacific engineer Theo C. Webster was piloting the eastbound train toward Deming, twenty miles to the east, when his fireman, who was leaning out of the locomotive cab and watching the track ahead, screamed out a warning: one of the rails was missing! Webster immediately applied the brakes, but before the train could stop, the locomotive, tender, and following three cars were derailed. The fireman, fearful that the boiler was about to explode, jumped from the cab. Webster, who was behind him, stepped up to the edge of the floor to jump when he was shot in the heart. He toppled out of the cab and onto the ground.

Charles Gaskill was a passenger on one of the derailed coaches. Curious, he leaned out of the coach window to determine what was going on and saw Webster fall. Gaskill climbed out of the coach and ran toward the engineer to render aid. Close on his heels was the conductor, Zach Vail. With all the confusion of the derailment, neither man had heard the shot that killed the engineer and had no idea that a robbery was about to take place. They got their first inkling when a man standing in the shadows hollered at them to stop and raise their hands. Both Gaskill and Vail were forced to hand over their money and valuables. The conductor had $200 on his person, fares he had earlier collected from the passengers. More robbers appeared out of the gloom.

With Gaskill and Vail neutralized, the bandits turned their attention to the derailed Wells, Fargo express car. One report stated there were five outlaws; another claimed seven. Inside, messenger T. G. Hodgekins offered little resistance as the robbers penetrated the door, entered the car, broke into the safe, and took an estimated $1,800. From the express car, they moved to the mail car but found nothing of value there. Having accomplished their goal, the robbers left the train, mounted their horses, and rode away to the north. Before leaving they shot and killed messenger Hodgekins.

Conductor Vail ran back to the passenger coaches to see if anyone was hurt. Discovering that the derailment had injured several badly, he ordered the brakeman, Tom Scott, to return to Gage Station and send a message to the sheriff's office in Deming requesting help. An hour after sunrise, a special train arrived at the scene transporting men and horses, a well-armed posse led by Luna County sheriff Harvey Whitehall. The tracks of the escaping robbers were located and followed for several miles before the posse lost them over an expanse of bare rock.

Whitehall suspected the gang of robbers consisted of a number of cowhands from the area of San Simon, Arizona. He advanced the notion that the engineer Webster would have known the men, explaining why he was killed. Other members of the posse believed the robbers were men who operated as the Gila Gang, also called the Cliffton (sometimes spelled Clifton) Gang, that operated out of a stronghold near the Gila River close to Pima, Arizona.

Shortly after the robbery, the Southern Pacific Railroad, along with the Wells, Fargo Express Company, offered rewards totaling $2,250. Several months later, Whitehall, acting on information he received, tracked down George Washington Cleveland (also spelled Cleavland) in Socorro, New Mexico. Whitehall convinced Cleveland that all his companions had been arrested and identified him as the man who shot and killed engineer Webster. Cleveland confessed to his part in the train robbery but denied firing the shot that killed the engineer. Before the interrogation was over, Cleveland had identified his fellow robbers.

George S. Collins, Kit Joy, and Mitch Lee were arrested a short time later at Socorro. Within a few days, Frank Taggert (also spelled Taggart) was arrested at Porte Cañon de Agua Frio near St. Thomas, Arizona. Within two weeks, all five robbers were in the jail at Silver City, New Mexico, under the supervision of Deputy Dick Ware.

On March 10, Lee and Taggert overpowered Ware while Joy relieved the deputy of his guns. With Ware subdued, the outlaws freed Cleveland, along with two other prisoners: Carlos Chavez and Charles Spencer. The outlaws ordered two jail guards to remove their shackles. Taking revolvers, a rifle, and a shotgun from an unlocked armory, the men, still dressed in jailhouse garb, fled. They ran straight for a local livery stable, where they stole horses. Cleveland selected an unbroken stallion, which threw him. Unable to control the animal, he was forced to ride double with one of his companions.

On learning of the jailbreak, Whitehall organized another posse and went in pursuit. He was joined by Silver City deputy sheriff F. C. Cantley and his posse. Santa Fe resident John C. Jackson had observed the prisoners fleeing from the jail. Before any of the lawmen could organize a posse, Jackson mounted his own horse and followed the outlaws from a distance, tracking them to the Fort Bayard Road and then north toward the Pinos Altos Mountains. On returning to Silver City, he encountered the lawmen on the trail and informed them of the route followed by the escapees.

The posse led by Cantley caught up with the train robbers at a pass in the Pinos Altos Mountains. Seeing that they were outnumbered and outgunned and that their pursuers had better mounts, the fugitives elected to make a stand. Cleveland was killed in the first volley of the ensuing firefight. Chavez was shot and killed a minute later. As the escapees scrambled for more suitable cover, Lee suffered a serious wound. Taggart ran out of ammunition and, seeing his companions fall to the lawmen's bullets, raised his hands in surrender, as did Spencer. Joy, though wounded, managed to escape and in the process shot and killed posse member Joe Laffer (also spelled La Fur).

Whitehall and his posse were all for hanging Lee, Taggart, and Spencer on the spot, but Cantley resisted. Ignoring Cantley, the posse men began searching for a suitable tree limb to which to attach their ropes. About that time, a US deputy marshal named Jenson arrived, so the posse put their planned execution on hold. One of the lawmen conversed with Jenson, suggesting that he ride to Fort Bayard, meet with the commanding officer, and determine what to do with the prisoners. Jenson agreed with the plan and rode away. As soon as he was out of sight, the posse men resumed their execution plans. Cantley continued to protest but was told in no uncertain terms that a hanging was about to take place. Cantley's guns were taken from him.

Taggart and Spencer had nooses placed around their necks and were given the time to say a few last words. Taggart admitted his role in the robbery but denied killing engineer Webster. He claimed Mitch Lee had done the shooting. Lee, standing next to Taggart, also denied it. As his noose was pulled tighter, he relented and admitted shooting the engineer. Moments later Lee and Taggart were dangling from their ropes. Spencer was spared.

Within the week, a Silver City coroner's jury declared that "the deceased came to their death by gunshot wounds and other injuries inflicted by the sheriff's posse and citizens while in pursuit." No mention was made of the hanging.

Kit Joy, though badly wounded from a bullet in his leg, made it to a ranch owned by Erichos Smith. Seeing the damage done to the limb, Smith amputated Joy's leg. Joy was eventually rearrested and tried for his role in the train robbery and as an accessory to the killing of engineer Webster. Convicted, he was sentenced to life in prison. Years later, however, he was released. He lived out the remainder of his life in Bisbee, Arizona.

During his time as a lawman, Harvey Whitehall earned a reputation as an effective deterrent to bad men. One of Whitehall's first moves after his election to the office of sheriff of Grant County, New Mexico, was to appoint noted gunman "Dangerous" Dan Tucker as deputy. Though numerous citizens railed against this decision, Whitehall, with Tucker's assistance, cleaned out the outlaw element in Silver City.

In 1875, Whitehall was the first lawman to arrest the outlaw Billy the Kid, who was then going by the alias William Bonney. The crimes: stealing cheese and stealing laundry. At one time, Pat Garrett, who claimed to have killed Billy the Kid, ran against Whitehall for sheriff of Grant County. Garrett, who was not well liked by many in New Mexico, was defeated soundly by Whitehall. Whitehall passed away in Deming on September 14, 1906.

CHAPTER 32

BLACK JACK KETCHUM

One of the most active and effective train robbers during the late 1800s was Thomas "Black Jack" Ketchum. After a number of train robbery successes in Colorado and Texas, Ketchum's gang was decimated, and he was on the run. To escape the pursuing lawmen, he made his way to New Mexico. He intended to hide out for a time but was now more determined than ever to rob trains, believing this was the quickest and easiest way to make money. He began making plans to rob the Colorado and Southern train as it approached the station at Folsom, New Mexico. Twice before, Ketchum had robbed this same train, and twice before he had succeeded. His third attempt was to be his last.

Ketchum never enjoyed the notoriety of the more prominent train robbers, such as Butch Cassidy, Jesse James, the Dalton Gang, the Doolin Gang, and others. He was, however, fearless and daring, regarded by many as far more violent and dangerous than any of the aforementioned. Along with his brother Sam, Black Jack Ketchum was wanted throughout much of Wyoming, Colorado, and Texas.

Ketchum was born near China Creek in San Saba County, Texas, on October 31, 1863. (One report states that he was born in 1866.) His father died when he was only five years old, and his mother, who was blind, passed away when he was ten. Young

Tom bounced around from one family member to another. An older brother, Green Berry Ketchum, was a successful farmer and breeder of horses. Another brother, Sam, was married with a family.

Still a young man, Tom left the Texas Hill Country and traveled west, determined to make it on his own. Brother Sam, lured by the prospects of adventure in some new territory, left his family and joined him. Together, the two found employment on ranches in West Texas and northern New Mexico and worked on a number of trail drives into Colorado and Wyoming.

After working menial and low-paying jobs, Ketchum decided on a career in outlawry. The possibility of making a lot of money by robbing trains immediately seized his attention, and he recruited several like-minded men. What became known as the Black Jack Ketchum Gang held up and robbed an Atchison, Topeka, and Santa Fe train near Deming, New Mexico, and got away with an estimated $20,000 (see chapter 34).

Over the next several years, the gang members, though preferring to rob trains and stagecoaches, were forced to find work from time to time on ranches. When the opportunity arose, however, they would resume their criminal activities. The gang was also responsible for a number of killings.

Tom's brother Sam often accompanied him on robberies. Over the years, researchers and writers have often confused the two, sometimes referring to Sam as "Black Jack." On occasion, both brothers rode with the famous Hole-in-the-Wall Gang that included Butch Cassidy, the Sundance Kid, Elzy Lay, Kid Curry, and other members of the Wild Bunch, all noted and proficient train robbers. There is little doubt that Black Jack Ketchum learned much about robbing trains from these gang members. By late 1895, Wild Bunch member Harvey "Kid Curry" Logan had become a member of Black Jack's gang.

All who came in contact with Ketchum regarded him as "crazy." He often exhibited behavior that was considered deranged and bizarre even by the standards of most hardened outlaws. Today, Ketchum would be referred to as a psychopath. The clearly disturbed Ketchum was considered far too outrageous, dangerous, and unpredictable even for most of the members of the Wild Bunch, themselves no strangers to violence and killing.

On a number of occasions, Ketchum was observed beating himself about the head with his own revolver and lashing himself across his back with his lariat. He explained that he was punishing himself for some mistake for which he determined he must be castigated. Once, when a woman Ketchum had been seeing decided she wanted no more to do with him, he beat himself bloody with the butt of his revolver in front of others.

Black Jack Ketchum was also known to drink heavily, sometimes with companions but more often alone. He would remain drunk for long periods, and as a result of his belligerence, bellicosity, and aggressiveness, his own gang members avoided him. Ketchum thought of himself as invincible, but his last train robbery proved that he wasn't.

CHAPTER 33

SOCORRO, OCTOBER 30, 1884

One October afternoon in Socorro, New Mexico, in 1884, five cowhands fell into a conversation about train robbery. Cowhand wages didn't amount to much, and they decided that robbing a train would yield greater wealth with a minimal time investment. The five were William Allen, Punch Collins, Jefferson Kirkendall (also spelled Kerkendall), J. W. Pointer, and Edwin White. None of the men had ever robbed a train before, and they would pay a price for their lack of experience.

One of the cowhands learned that the Santa Fe No. 102 would be arriving at the Socorro station at a certain time, carrying passengers and pulling an express car, all of which could be robbed. The five men decided to force the train to a halt and hold it up at a location about five miles out of Socorro. At first they tried to unbolt one of the rails and move it aside in order to cause the train to leave the tracks. Not having the appropriate tools to accomplish this, however, they decided instead to pile rocks on the tracks, creating what they believed was an impassible obstacle. Such a technique had long been used to stop trains for the purpose of robbery. An obstruction such as a pile of large rocks or items such as railroad ties could in fact derail a train. Playing it safe, most engineers would stop on spotting such an obstacle.

The five cowhands piled a long line of large rocks on the tracks, climbed down the banked railroad bed to find a place

of concealment, and waited for the train. Two hours later, the
Santa Fe could be heard rumbling in the distance. The cowhands
checked their revolvers and readied themselves for the moment the
train stopped.

The engineer on the Santa Fe No. 2 was an experienced, longtime railroad employee named James Skuse. When Skuse spotted
the pile of rocks ahead on the tracks, he did the only logical thing:
he applied the brakes, moved the throttle into reverse, and slowed
the train. As it creaked to a stop before the rock obstruction, Skuse
saw five men carrying revolvers scurrying up the railroad embankment and headed for the locomotive cab. Each wore a bandanna
across his face with eyeholes cut into it.

Punch Collins climbed into the locomotive and held his handgun on Skuse and the fireman. Pointer and Allen had been sent
to the coaches with the intent of keeping the passengers and other
railroad employees from exiting the cars. White and Kirkendall
broke into the express car with little difficulty and began rummaging through its contents. Unable to find anything of value in the
express car, the bandits regrouped outside the train and argued
about whether to try the mail car or go rob the passengers.

As the debate continued, engineer Skuse told the fireman to
walk ahead of the locomotive and begin removing the bigger rocks.
Before he could do so, however, he was spotted by Kirkendall and
White and ordered back into the locomotive.

Skuse turned his gaze back to the rock pile on the tracks
ahead, came to a conclusion, and made a decision. None of the
rocks seemed particularly large, and with the cowcatcher on the
front of the engine, Skuse believed the train could plow through
the blockage. While the train robbers were otherwise occupied,
Skuse grabbed the throttle, pulled it wide open, and started the
train through the rocks ahead. The cowcatcher had no difficulty
pushing the obstacles to the side, and as the train tore through
the obstruction, the bandits fired their weapons at the departing
locomotive and cars but did little damage. Frustrated by their

failure, they walked over to where they had tied their horses and rode away.

The five cowhands were not prepared for what happened next. Since the robbery attempt had failed, they presumed there would be no pursuit. They were wrong. In a short time they were identified. Collins, Kirkendall, Pointer, and White were arrested with little difficulty. Allen fled to another state and was never apprehended.

CHAPTER 34

NUTT, 1892

Black Jack Ketchum's first train robbery took place at Nutt, a station providing water and fuel for Atchison, Topeka, and Santa Fe trains. Today, Nutt is a mere memory, and even the remains of the station are hard to find. In 1892, it was located some twenty miles north of Deming, New Mexico. Since Deming was the closest significant railroad depot, the event has often been referred to as the Deming train robbery. Press coverage was scarce to nonexistent, and few particulars are known. Even the actual date of the robbery has been lost.

Black Jack Ketchum, his brother Sam, and several other members of Black Jack's gang learned that an Atchison, Topeka, and Santa Fe train was en route to Deming. Inside the express car, according to the scant reports available, was a shipment of $20,000 in cash. After the train stopped at Nutt, the gang members, wearing masks and wielding revolvers, had little difficulty subduing the engineer, the fireman, and the express car messenger.

As the robbery was taking place, the conductor slipped off the train and made his way into the station, where he telegraphed for help. Within minutes of receiving the telegram, a lawman in Lake Valley, eighteen miles north of Nutt, was organizing a posse and preparing to head south to the scene. The posse was too far away to be of much assistance. By the time it had arrived, Black Jack and his gang were miles away. A few days later, the robbers crossed the border into Arizona. For a time their identities were unknown, but the subsequent investigation turned its attention toward Black Jack Ketchum. The $20,000 taken from the express car was never recovered.

CHAPTER 35

BLACK JACK CHRISTIAN

William "Black Jack" Christian was born in Fort Griffin, Texas, on September 5, 1871. Because they followed a similar path of criminal activity, including train robbery, as well as a nickname, Christian and another outlaw—Thomas "Black Jack" Ketchum— are sometimes confused with each other. There is no evidence that the two ever met.

Little is known of Christian's youth save for the fact that he and his brother Bob traveled westward into New Mexico and Arizona, where they fell into outlawry—cattle rustling at first, then robbery. Christian's name, along with that of his brother, can be found in documents and newspaper reports related to criminal activity beginning in the late 1880s. Around that time, Christian, a big man with a large frame, acquired his first nickname, "202," said to be a reference to his weight. According to writers, he later acquired the nickname "Black Jack" for his short and bad temper.

During the late 1880s and early 1890s, both Christian brothers organized what was referred to as the High Fives Gang and conducted robberies throughout much of New Mexico Territory. In 1895, the two brothers were in Guthrie, Oklahoma, where they shot and killed William C. Turner, a lawman. They were arrested one month later and placed in the Oklahoma County jail but managed to escape. The brothers eventually made their way to Arizona Territory. On August 6, 1896, the High Fives Gang robbed the

William "Black Jack" Christian

International Bank at Nogales, Arizona. During their escape, gang member Jess Williams, who was carrying the loot, suffered a bullet wound that caused him to drop it.

By now, the High Fives Gang was referred to as the Black Jack Christian Gang. As a result of confusion among newspaper writers, both William and Bob were referred to as "Black Jack," and each of them may have employed the nickname at various times.

At this point William Christian was a successful robber of banks and stores. He began to set his sights on greater targets and decided that train robbery would yield greater loot. He decided the gang should rob the eastbound Atlantic and Pacific train near Rio Puerco, New Mexico.

CHAPTER 36

RIO PUERCO, OCTOBER 2, 1896

About thirty-five miles southwest of Albuquerque, New Mexico, lies a location known during the 1880s as Rio Puerco, the name of a nearby river given to a small railroad station established there. The remains of ancient Indian villages have been found throughout the Rio Puerco River valley. Few of them were permanent, however, for the river has a history of flooding. To this day, settlement along this part of the river is rare. In 1892, the Atlantic and Pacific Railroad ran tracks through the region. Trains stopped at the Rio Puerco station to take on water and fuel.

Around sundown on the evening of October 2, 1896, the Atlantic and Pacific eastbound run encountered a crank pin problem a few miles west of the station. Crank pins, also called crank journals, are the parts of a shaft that rest on bearings at the ends of the connecting rods opposite the pistons. Engineer Charles Ross pulled the train to a stop in order to address the problem. Following an inspection, he decided to try to take the train to the Rio Puerco station, where he would make the necessary adjustments. Sam Heady, the conductor, stepped forward and advised that he did not believe the train would get much farther down the track with the problem and advised Ross to fix it then and there. Since the conductor has greater authority than the engineer, Ross retrieved his tools and with the assistance of the fireman set to work on the crank pin.

The problem turned out to be minor, and within ten minutes Ross and the fireman were climbing back into the locomotive cab and preparing to continue down the track. Just as the train pulled away and was beginning to pick up speed, two men carrying revolvers ran toward the locomotive and jumped aboard. A brakeman witnessed the event and shouted at the intruders. One of them fired several shots at the brakeman. A bullet struck his lantern; a second one wounded him in the hand. Ross, surprised at the appearance of the newcomers and witnessing the commotion, immediately applied the brakes.

Inside the express car, messenger L. J. Kohler heard the gunshots and felt the train come to a stop once again. Fearing a robbery, Kohler doused the express car lantern, armed himself with a self-cocking revolver, and prepared for whatever might happen next.

Inside the first coach behind the express car, one of the passengers also suspected a robbery was taking place. He was US Deputy Marshal Will Loomis. Loomis grabbed his shotgun and sent a newsboy selling papers on the train to fetch the shells out of his travel bag stacked at the end of the coach.

As Loomis was loading the shells into his shotgun, Kohler listened for the approach of the outlaws outside the express car. The bandits had forced the engineer and fireman out of the cab and marched them down the track toward the car. On arriving, messenger Kohler could hear the outlaws instructing the engineer to uncouple the express car from the rest of the train. To Kohler it sounded like the robbers were milling around just outside the door. Deciding to take the offensive, he fired several shots through the wooden door in the hope of striking one or more of the robbers.

About this same time, Marshal Loomis made his way to the rear platform of the passenger coach and leaned off to the side, looking toward the express car. He spotted several men in a cluster just outside the express car but was unable to distinguish the robbers from the train crew. As his eyes adjusted to the dimming light, he watched as one man stepped away from the others. Loomis identified the man as a robber, raised his shotgun, and fired a load of buckshot. The train robber was knocked to the ground, cursing. Clearly wounded, the outlaw struggled to his feet and fired two shots from his revolver at Loomis. Both missed, and the deputy marshal once again calmly raised his shotgun, pointed it at his target, and fired the second load of buckshot. Struck again, the unlucky train robber dropped to the ground and rolled down the embankment into a ditch below. The dead man was later identified as Cole Young.

Loomis stepped back into the passenger coach to reload his shotgun. He hoped he wouldn't need it. He considered that the robbers, discouraged by the death of one of their companions, might move on. He was wrong. As he placed shells into the chamber, Loomis heard the sound of the express car being uncoupled from the rest of the train and the robbers yelling at the engineer to pull ahead. Loomis jumped out of the coach just as the locomotive was picking up speed. Unseen by the bandits, he raced to the express car, jumped onto the rear platform, and hung on as the train chugged down the track. Several minutes later, it slowed dramatically as it approached a trestle.

Just before the train pulled to a stop, Loomis, still carrying his shotgun, jumped from the express car platform and positioned himself on the opposite side, where he was less likely to be spotted. As he waited in the shadows for the robbers to reappear, he could hear the outlaws deciding that pursuit would be less likely if they got to the other side of the trestle. With that, the train started up again and moved forward. Loomis scrambled to regain his position at the back of the express car. Once the train stopped again on the other side of the trestle, he jumped off.

The robbers returned once again to the express car. They called for the messenger to open the door, but Kohler resisted. The train robbers were ill prepared, having brought neither tools with which to pry open the door nor dynamite with which to blow it open. By this time, nearly an hour had passed since the train was first boarded and stopped. As messenger Kohler listened through the door, he could hear the growing level of frustration among the bandits. Discouraged by this turn of events, as well as the death of Cole Young, they simply walked away.

As with most train robberies, an investigation followed. The foiled robbers were identified as members of the Black Jack Christian Gang led by either Bob or Will Christian, a notorious band of outlaws who counted robbing trains among their numerous criminal skills.

CHAPTER 37

GRANTS, NOVEMBER 6, 1897

The engineer of the eastbound Atlantic and Pacific No. 2 had just pulled into the water stop at Grants, New Mexico, one hour before sundown on November 6, 1897. Grants lies sixty miles west of Albuquerque. As was his practice, the engineer, H. D. McCarthy, climbed down from the cab and, along with the fireman, Henry Abel, conducted a quick inspection of the locomotive. Assured that everything was in order, Abel climbed back into the cab while McCarthy stepped onto the small station platform and became engaged in a conversation with the conductor, a man named Aldrich. The two men were suddenly interrupted by gunfire. As McCarthy and Aldrich watched, three men wearing masks and carrying revolvers scrambled aboard the locomotive and into the cab.

At gunpoint, the newcomers ordered fireman Abel to pull the train forward and said he would be instructed where to stop the train a mile or so down the track. Abel's worst fears were being realized: the train was being robbed. Just as the No. 2 pulled away from the station, McCarthy and Aldrich jumped from the station platform onto the blind of one of the passenger coaches.

A few minutes later, Abel pulled the train to a halt well beyond the town limits and near a row of livestock pens. The outlaws climbed down from the cab and, along with Abel, walked back to the express car. There, they told Abel to uncouple the express car from the rest of the train. The outlaws accompanied Abel back to

171

the locomotive, where they ordered him to pull the train forward another mile. McCarthy and Aldrich were left behind.

On this particular run, there was no messenger assigned to the express car. When the train pulled into a station where packages needed to be unloaded, an express company representative assigned to the station would come out to the car, unlock it with his key, and retrieve the necessary deliveries.

When the train had stopped once again, the outlaws made their way back to the express car and found a locked door. As the sliding door was substantial, the car was not easy to break into. Furthermore, the robbers did not have the necessary tools to do so. They had something more effective: dynamite. One of the outlaws attached a large charge to the heavy door, lit a fuse, and advised the others to take cover. When the smoke had cleared from the explosion, the outlaws were stunned to discover it had inflicted very little damage to the door. Another charge was applied, and like the first, this one had minimal effect.

For the third attempt, the outlaws applied a much larger charge of dynamite to the door. After lighting the fuse, the outlaws, as well as fireman Abel, once again took cover. The resulting explosion blew apart the entire side and one end of the express car.

As the western New Mexico winds carried away the smoke from the blast, two of the robbers entered the smoldering car and searched for the safe. A few moments later they found it: a heavy, steel Wells, Fargo safe. Another significant charge of dynamite was taped to the safe and detonated. The door was blown off and the contents within exposed. In only a few moments, the outlaws scooped out an estimated $100,000 in gold and silver coins. These they stuffed into their saddlebags, which they then loaded onto horses tied nearby. The leader of the train robbers bid fireman Abel a polite goodnight and led his followers away into the growing darkness.

Abel made a mental note of the direction the fleeing outlaws took. He then ran back to the express car, which by now had burst into flames. Feeling a responsibility to save the packages inside the ruined car, Abel decided to return the train to the station at Grants as fast as he could. As he backed up the train, he was unable to see much behind him because of the smoke and flames from the express car. Before he was aware of the proximity of the rest of the decoupled train, he rammed into it, crushing the lead passenger coach and the one immediately behind it. Fortunately, almost all the passengers had left the coach when the outlaws had the locomotive and express car pulled forward. Many of them were walking back to the station when the accident occurred.

The few passengers who chose to remain in the coaches, though startled, were uninjured and quickly climbed to the ground. Moments later, both coaches caught fire from the burning express car.

As soon as was possible, Abel returned what was left of the train to the station at Grants. After wiring the railroad company as well as area law enforcement authorities of the holdup, Abel remained at the station, where he was joined the following afternoon by a contingent of Wells, Fargo agents, railroad detectives, the Cibola County sheriff, and several men who were deputized specifically for the anticipated pursuit. Abel told the lawmen that the outlaws rode away in a southerly direction toward the lava beds.

The lawmen were discouraged by this news. The lava beds, or *malpais*, as the Mexican residents of the area called them, were a vast expanse of ancient and weathered basaltic rock from eons-old volcanic eruptions. It was a rugged environment, water was scarce, and twisting, turning, and dead-end trails favored men on the run. Travelers and hunters who entered the *malpais* were sometimes never seen again.

In all, fifteen men made up the posse. They followed the tracks of the train robbers for three days before losing the trail in the lava beds. They gave up and returned to Grants. It was later learned that the posse had passed within one hundred yards of the outlaws' camp without realizing it.

During their flight from the scene of the robbery, the outlaws rode hard, following trails through the *malpais*, with which they were familiar. Deep in the confines of this rugged landscape, they stopped at an old Indian campsite they had used before. There, they found a freshwater spring and adequate protection from the unceasing and often harsh desert winds. Importantly to the train robbers, the site also afforded an excellent defensive position should pursuing lawmen track them there.

The morning following the train robbery, the outlaws prepared a meal of bacon cooked over a low campfire and drank from a bottle of whiskey. They celebrated their successful heist. The three men drank heavily for the next two hours, and by mid-morning they were all drunk. Soon they fell to arguing over the division of the gold and silver coins.

One of the outlaws, angered by a perceived insult from another, pulled his revolver from his holster and shot his antagonist through the head, killing him instantly. Hours later when the two remaining outlaws sobered up, they dug a hole to bury their dead companion. As they were about to carry the corpse to the hole, they heard the sounds of men and horses passing along a nearby trail. It was the posse that had earlier ridden out of Grants. The two outlaws climbed to an elevated knob and spotted the riders no more than one hundred yards away. Scurrying back to the campsite, they decided that in order to effect an unimpeded flight from the lawmen, they needed to cache the loot from the train robbery. They tossed the treasure-laden saddlebags into the hole they had recently dug and laid the body of the dead man on top of them. After refilling the hole, they mounted their horses and rode southward and out of the lava beds.

The next morning, the leader of the two suggested they split up in order to confuse pursuit. They agreed to meet in Silver City, New Mexico, in thirty days. From there, they would return to the campsite and retrieve the gold and silver coins.

After returning to Grants, the search party obtained enough information to identify the robbers as Black Jack Christian and two members of his gang. A substantial reward was offered for the outlaw, dead or alive, but few were willing to enter the forbidding *malpais* to search for him.

Two weeks later, Black Jack Christian tried to rob another train near Silver City, New Mexico. He was badly wounded and barely escaped. A few days later, his companion tried to rob a train in eastern Arizona. He was subdued and arrested, tried and found guilty, and sentenced to twenty years in the Yuma Territorial Prison. He died from consumption after serving only five.

Christian lived for only two days following his aborted train robbery attempt. Before he died, he was arrested by the Catron County sheriff. One evening, as the sheriff visited his cell, Christian confessed to robbing the Atlantic and Pacific No. 2 near Grants. He also related the events at the hidden campsite in the *malpais*, along with the killing of a fellow outlaw and the burying of the gold and silver coins. As the sheriff prompted him, Christian described the site of the cache and provided vague directions.

A week after Christian died, the sheriff, accompanied by deputies, led an expedition into the lava beds in search of the cache. He found Christian's directions confusing, and the lawmen became lost several times. They returned empty-handed. The sheriff led a second expedition several weeks later with the same result. Frustrated, he finally gave up.

During the summer of 1904, an out-of-work cowhand was traveling through the lava beds. He made camp one evening in a grassy area in the shelter of a secluded rock overhang. From a nearby spring he obtained fresh water for his horse and for his coffee. As he was bringing his coffee to a boil over the campfire, the cowhand noticed a low mound of dirt several feet from where he squatted. It looked like a grave, but one that had not been excavated and refilled with care. It did not appear to be very old. Curious, he walked over to it. Growing more curious, he dug into it, and only a few inches into the ground he found a skeleton, decaying flesh, and rotted clothes. Spooked by his discovery, he quickly refilled the hole and returned to his coffee. Had the cowhand removed the skeleton and dug another inch or two into the ground, he would have encountered a fortune well beyond his wildest dreams.

Years later, when the cowhand was an old man with grandchildren, he heard story of the Grants train robbery by the outlaw Black Jack Christian and his gang, along with the deathbed tale of the location of the buried loot. He realized that he had found the site of the treasure cache decades earlier without knowing it.

Over the course of the next two years, the old cowhand undertook several trips into the *malpais* in the hope that he could relocate that same campsite, the one that had the freshwater spring and offered sanctuary from the desiccating desert winds. He died without ever finding it. The great fortune in gold and silver, worth millions of dollars today, still lies there in a shallow grave beneath the skeleton of the long-dead train robber.

His story of finding the grave with the skeleton, coupled with the tale of Black Jack Christian's robbery of the Atlantic and Pacific train, has lured hopeful treasure hunters into the dangerous *malpais* in search of the cache. To date, there is no report that anyone has found it. The search continues.

Addendum

There exists an alternate version of the death of Black Jack Christian. At least one writer is convinced that Christian was killed during a shootout with a posse in what today is called Black Jack Canyon near Clifton, Arizona, on April 28, 1897, seven months prior to robbery of the Atlantic and Pacific No. 2 train near Grants, New Mexico. According to this account, four members of the gang, including Black Jack Christian, were passing through a small canyon when a posse waiting in ambush killed them. The dead bodies were transported into town atop the load in a lumber wagon and placed on display. Though it was claimed one of the outlaws was Black Jack Christian, evidence is lacking.

CHAPTER 38

FOLSOM, AUGUST 16, 1899

By April 16, 1899, Thomas "Black Jack" Ketchum had been hiding out for several weeks in New Mexico, to which he had escaped after being pursued by Texas lawmen. Wanted in Texas for train robbery, he felt relatively safe in his new location. Maintaining a low profile for a time would have been in his best interest, but the unpredictable and impulsive Ketchum could not resist the opportunity to rob another train. As he lacked adequate preparation, this urge led to what would be his last train robbery and, ultimately, his demise.

Ketchum was somewhat familiar with the schedules of the Colorado and Southern Railroad line in northeastern New Mexico; he, along with his gang, had robbed the company's trains in the past. Ketchum, however, was without a gang. Rather than take the time and effort to assemble one, he decided to undertake the challenge by himself. By this time the deranged Ketchum had long since entered into the realm of madness and instability. The historical record shows that train robbery attempts executed by a single bandit were rarely successful.

Ketchum rode to a location not far from the Colorado and Southern station at Folsom, a lonely spot along the route from Raton to Clayton. After looking over the station and the tiny settlement nearby, he rode some distance away into a shallow canyon, where he spent the night in a cave. Early the next morning

177

he saddled his horse, mounted up, and rode back toward Folsom. At this early hour, everything was quiet save for the chuffing of the eastbound Colorado and Southern locomotive at the station platform as it prepared to depart. Other than one man loading a small amount of freight into one of the cars, few were about, and Ketchum went unnoticed. After reaching a point behind the station, he dismounted, turned his horse loose, and observed the goings-on near the train.

Moments before the Colorado and Southern was to leave, Ketchum dashed from behind the station, crossed the tracks, and boarded the train from the blind side of the baggage car. As the train pulled away, Ketchum climbed to the top of the car and made his way forward. He reached a point atop the coal tender where he waited until the train was approximately three miles from the station. When convinced sufficient distance had been covered, Ketchum crawled to the front of the tender and dropped into the locomotive cab. Pointing his revolver in the face of the surprised and frightened engineer, the outlaw ordered the train stopped.

After the train was halted, Ketchum forced the engineer out of the cab and marched him back to the express and mail cars. He planned to have the engineer uncouple the cars from the rest of the train and pull forward another mile up the track. There the train would be stopped once again, and Ketchum, at his leisure, would break into the express and baggage cars and rob them without any interference from the passengers in the trailing coaches. For reasons unknown, Ketchum was uncomfortable with the location of the first stop, and before uncoupling the cars had the engineer pull forward another mile.

Ketchum erred in his decision as to where to stop. The train was on a tight curve and in a somewhat cramped position, making it impossible to uncouple the cars. Disappointed but undeterred, Ketchum climbed out of the cab and walked down to the cars he targeted. Selecting the express car, he broke in, having encountered no resistance whatsoever from the messenger. One account of the robbery has the always volatile Ketchum shooting the express messenger in the jaw. Another account states that this did not happen.

With the train stopping, starting up again, and then stopping once more, the conductor, Frank Harrington, grew convinced that a robbery was in progress. A veteran of at least three previous robberies, Harrington had lost patience with outlaws and was determined never to be held up again. Peering out a coach window, he discerned that only one robber was involved. The conductor retrieved his shotgun, climbed out of the coach, and went after the bandit.

Ketchum had gone through the express car and found nothing worth taking. He moved on to the baggage car. When Harrington arrived at the baggage car, he could hear the robber rummaging around inside. The conductor stepped to the door, aimed his shotgun at the robber, and ordered him to desist. Reacting to this unexpected threat, Ketchum yanked his revolver from its holster and got off a hurried shot at the intruder. The bullet whizzed by Harrington's head, missing him by an inch. (Another account has Harrington being wounded by the shot.) Harrington responded to the assault by firing back at the robber.

The load of buckshot struck Ketchum in the right elbow, nearly severing his lower arm. Ketchum staggered and fell out of the baggage car onto the ground. Harrington yelled for the engineer to get the train moving as fast as possible. As the engineer manned the throttle, Harrington climbed aboard the open baggage car and, as the train sped away, watched the wounded train robber, clearly in pain, make his way to the shelter of some trees a short distance from the tracks.

The brave and daring conductor Harrington saved the train from being robbed. Little did he know at the time that the man he shot was the notorious train robber Black Jack Ketchum. Harrington would learn several days later that he was responsible to putting an end to Ketchum's criminal career.

CHAPTER 39

THE END OF BLACK JACK KETCHUM

After attempting to rob the eastbound Colorado and Southern train near Folsom, New Mexico, on August 16, 1899, Black Jack Ketchum had to show for his effort only a severe wound to his right arm, the lower part dangling from the upper by tendons and sinew. Dizzy and in great pain, Ketchum collapsed to the ground near the railroad tracks and waited for the inevitable posse to arrive.

The engineer for the Colorado and Southern train stopped at every station along his route and had telegraphs describing the robbery attempt sent to law enforcement authorities at a number of locations. The messages advised them to be on the lookout for a badly wounded man near the location of the scene of the botched holdup. By the time the train pulled into the station at Clayton, New Mexico, the sheriff was in the process of forming a posse. Within minutes, it was racing back toward the scene of the robbery fifty miles away. On arriving, however, the wounded man could not be found.

Earlier, fearing he was dying from his wound, Ketchum had flagged down another train. When the train came to a stop, the brakeman spotted the lone individual, clearly in distress, near the tracks. He climbed down and approached the injured stranger, prepared to provide aid. To his shock, the man pulled his revolver and pointed it at his chest. A conductor arrived at the scene, took it all in, and said to the stranger, "We just came to help you, but if this is the way you feel we will go and leave you."

Barely able to stand, Ketchum lowered his weapon. He told the brakeman that he was "all done" and to "take me in." The brakeman and the conductor lifted Ketchum into the caboose and placed him on a cot. The conductor summoned a guard to remain in the caboose with him as the train proceeded toward Folsom. On arriving, Ketchum was placed under arrest by Union County sheriff Saturnino Pinard, who had been informed of the earlier robbery attempt.

On being entered into the arrest log, Ketchum gave his name as Frank Stevens. (One writer claims he provided the name George Stevens.) With the limited resources available at Folsom, Ketchum's wound was cleaned and bandaged. Forty-two shotgun pellets were plucked out of his arm. As soon as it was possible to do so, the train robber was transported to San Raphael Hospital in Trinidad, Colorado, forty-five miles to the northwest. There, what remained of his forearm was amputated.

During the subsequent investigation, lawmen learned that Frank Stevens was, in truth, the notorious train robber Thomas "Black Jack" Ketchum, a man wanted in New Mexico since 1892. It was also learned that Ketchum was wanted in four other states for train robbery, bank robbery, murder, and more. When deemed by his doctor to be well enough to travel, Ketchum was moved to Santa Fe, where he was kept in a cell pending trial. During the time he was incarcerated in Santa Fe, Ketchum confessed to inter-rogators his roles in a number of previous holdups in Texas, even to the point of providing details of the planning and execution of his crimes.

After the passage of a few weeks, Ketchum was transferred to Clayton, where he was formally charged with the attempted robbery of the Colorado and Southern train near Folsom. He was tried, found guilty, and sentenced to be hanged. While in jail, Ketchum was given the opportunity to meet with a priest, but the unrepentant outlaw said, "I'm gonna die as I've lived, and you ain't gonna change me in a few minutes." To this he added, "Have someone play a fiddle when I swing off." The priest was sent away.

The execution was set for April 26, 1901, at 8:00 a.m. Black Jack Ketchum wore a suit. He was heavily manacled, and a heavy steel belt encircled his waist, his good arm cuffed to the belt. His legs were linked together with a short length of chain such that he could only shuffle forward. He was escorted by several deputies, all carrying rifles. These impressive precautions seemed rather unnecessary for a one-armed man who was barely able to move, but the sheriff was reacting to rumors that members of the Black Jack Ketchum Gang would arrive and attempt to free the captive.

Within a few seconds after Ketchum had ascended the steps of the gallows, a black hood was fitted over his head and pinned to his shirt. As the hangman on the platform secured the noose around his neck, Ketchum, in a taunting manner, said, "Hurry up, boys. Get this over with. I'll be in hell before you start breakfast, boys!" Following some final adjustments to the noose, Ketchum yelled, "Let 'er rip!"

Clayton sheriff Salome Garcia stood by with a hatchet to sever the rope that released the trapdoor through which Ketchum would drop. The job required two blows. As the trap door swung open, Ketchum dropped through the opening, his body plummeting toward the ground. When the limit of the rope was reached, the outlaw's head was torn off. The body dropped to the ground, and the head, after swinging for a moment on the rope, fell and landed atop the torso and then bounced to the ground. Onlookers screamed, and photographers rushed forward to record the grisly scene. Black Jack Ketchum's train robbery days were officially over. Later that day, Ketchum's remains were interred in the Clayton cemetery.

CHAPTER 40

LOGAN, JULY 30, 1904

Logan is a small village in northeastern New Mexico located thirty miles northeast of Tucumcari on US Highway 54 and about twenty miles west of the border with Texas. Established when the Chicago, Rock Island, and Pacific Railroad constructed a bridge over the nearby Canadian River, the town was named for Eugene Logan, a former Texas Ranger who worked on the bridge. Today, the Union Pacific Railroad Company continues to run trains through Logan, which still maintains a small siding. Today, its population is just over one thousand residents.

On the evening of July 30, 1904, a Chicago, Rock Island, and Pacific passenger train pulled into the station at Logan. Following the unloading and loading of mail and freight, an inspection of the engine, and a short break for the passengers, the train was preparing to pull out when several men wearing masks and pointing handguns entered one of the passenger coaches. The number of train robbers reported ranges from three to seven.

The conductor, John York, stepped forward to lodge a protest and was immediately shot in the leg. Once passengers, conductor, engineer, and other railroad personnel were overpowered or otherwise rendered harmless, the robbers enlisted some assistance to uncouple the express car from the rest of the train. This done, the engineer was instructed to pull the train one mile down the track and stop. When the train had halted, the outlaws turned their attention to the express car. After breaking in, they located two safes—an express safe and a local safe. Anticipating that no one aboard the train was carrying keys or combinations to these safes, the outlaws were prepared to blow them open with dynamite. This was where their problems began.

By 1904, a technique wherein both safes could be blown open with a minimum of effort had served train robbers well on numerous occasions. On this attempt, however, it created problems. The technique was to place the smaller local safe atop the larger express safe, sometimes called the "through safe." In the space between the bottom of the local safe and the top of the express safe a charge of dynamite was wedged close to the doors of each. If everything went according to plan, the resulting blast would neatly blow the doors off both safes. The secret lay in the amount of dynamite used. The robbers of the Rock Island train were unskilled in the use of dynamite.

The safes were stacked and the dynamite placed. When the fuse was lit, the robbers took cover. The resulting blast accomplished nothing more than blowing the smaller safe through the roof of the express car and several yards out into the desert brush alongside the tracks. The door of neither safe was impacted. After retrieving the local safe and placing it once again atop the express safe, the robbers applied another charge, this one somewhat larger than the first. This time, the explosion blew the small safe through the side of the express car.

A quick inspection revealed that, as with the first charge, the doors of both safes were unaffected save for some burn marks. A third attempt was in order, but the outlaws discovered they had used the last of their dynamite on the second charge. Foiled and disappointed, the would-be train robbers walked away from the damaged express car.

A subsequent investigation suggested that the hopeful train robbers were members of a gang that had ridden down from Colorado. No attempt was made to track them, and their identities were never learned.

CHAPTER 41

DEMING, NOVEMBER 24, 1937

On November 24, 1937, Henry Loftus and Harry Donaldson were riding together in a westbound Southern Pacific passenger coach. The train, called the Apache Limited, had departed the station at El Paso, Texas, nearly an hour earlier. Unbeknownst to the passengers, both Loftus and Donaldson carried large revolvers and were intent on robbing the train.

Loftus was born Henry Lorenz in Manitowoc, Wisconsin, to German immigrant parents. As a teenager, he remained bored except when reading dime novels about western adventures and outlaws. His parents referred to this as his "Wild West complex" and assumed he would outgrow it. In his late teens, young Lorenz was arrested for burglary, but a sympathetic judge just placed him on probation.

In 1936, Lorenz's father moved to Chicago and purchased a shoe store. Henry remained only for a few months before deciding to travel to Brooklyn, New York, in search of adventure. He lasted in the big city for only a short time before announcing to one and all that he was heading west because that was where, he believed, his destiny lay. On his trip west he was accompanied by Donaldson. Donaldson was from Canada and had met Lorenz in Brooklyn. The two shared the same eagerness to explore the American West.

The two men traveled from place to place, eventually winding up in El Paso, a location both had heard about. Somewhere along his travels, Lorenz changed his name to Loftus. On arriving, however, the two were disappointed to see that the era of outlaws and shootings in the West Texas frontier that they had read about had long since passed. In 1936, El Paso was a modern city with tall buildings, paved streets and highways, a lot of automobiles, and very few horses. Undeterred, the two city boys from the North spent much of the money they had on what they thought were cowboy clothes, including fringed chaps and ten-gallon hats.

To the El Paso residents, the newcomers looked ridiculous, but the laughter and jeers did nothing to dissuade them. They purchased two horses along with saddles and other necessary gear, mounted up, and rode across the desert from El Paso northwestward toward Deming, New Mexico. Two days later, they arrived at this small railroad and ranching town and once more faced the reality that the Wild West they had read so much about no longer existed. Deciding to do something about it, the two men sold their horses and gear and with the proceeds purchased two six-shooters along with fancy hand-tolled holsters. With their remaining funds, they purchased two train tickets back to El Paso. Along the way they decided to rob the train.

As the Southern Pacific Apache Limited left the station at Deming, Loftus raised himself up in his seat, pulled his handgun from beneath his jacket, and pointed it at the conductor, W. M. Holloway. Initially, Holloway thought Loftus was drunk and pulling a prank. He commented later that because Loftus's hands were shaking so badly, he feared the gun might go off by accident. Holloway's worst fears were realized, however, when Loftus continued to point the gun at him while Donaldson, his own gun in hand, went from passenger to passenger taking the men's watches but, oddly, none of their money.

One of the passengers, a highly nervous man, made a sudden move that startled Donaldson. Already nervous himself, Donaldson panicked and shot the man in the hip. Loftus, on witnessing the disturbance, rushed toward Donaldson to assist when he was tackled by W. L. Smith, a railroad brakeman who happened to be riding as a passenger. Smith and Loftus were locked in a wrestling match on the floor of the car when the revolver went off, killing the brakeman.

A moment later, a number of passengers leaped from their seats and attacked the two train robbers, showing them no mercy and beating them nearly to death. Several of the female passengers called for the attackers to cease. Loftus and Donaldson were tied to their seats, and when the Southern Pacific arrived in Deming, they were turned over to the sheriff. Arrested and charged with train robbery and murder, the two men were sent to Las Cruces, New Mexico, for trial.

In Las Cruces, District Attorney Martin Threet, amid voiced concerns that the two prisoners were unfit to stand trial, entered not guilty pleas on their behalf. On learning of his incarceration, Loftus's father and sister traveled from Chicago to Las Cruces to be with him. As much as support from his family, Loftus needed money to help with his defense. The father and sister were unable to provide any but said they would return for the trial if possible. Donaldson's mother traveled from Nova Scotia to be with her son.

If the two men pled not guilty and the case went to trial, if found guilty they could get the death penalty Facing that situation, both men pleaded guilty to second-degree murder. In February, following a short trial, Loftus and Donaldson were both sentenced to fifty to seventy-five years in prison.

The botched Deming train robbery received national attention. The press called it "the last major train robbery in the United States" and said that the two convicted men were "the last of America's classic train robbers." The press erred on both counts. It was not a successful robbery; in fact, it failed miserably. And the two men—Loftus and Donaldson—were not classic train robbers, merely two bumbling wannabe outlaws who knew little to nothing about crime or robbery other than what they had read in paperback novels.

WYOMING

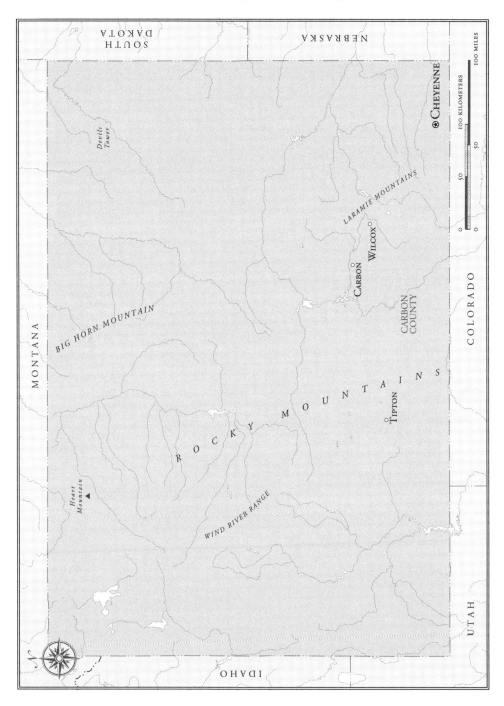

CHAPTER 42

CARBON, JUNE 2, 1878

Though not primarily known as a train robber, George "Big Nose" Parrott is widely regarded as one of the most colorful outlaws to undertake such an endeavor. To be more specific, Parrott never actually robbed a train; he only attempted to do so. Oddly, Parrott became famous long after he was dead.

Parrott was primarily a small-time cattle rustler who operated out of Wyoming. His opportunity to become involved with robbing a train came about when he fell in with the outlaw Frank James, who, during the 1870s, had arrived in the Powder River region of Wyoming. There he met Parrott and, as he was looking to recruit some help in robbing a train, enlisted him and a handful of his gang members. Parrott, for his part, was determined to learn the rudiments of train robbery from the famous bad man.

James, who was using the alias McKinney, operated mostly in the background as the planner of the robbery and placed Parrott in charge of pulling off the heist. The westbound Union Pacific No. 3 was selected and the best place to stop it, reasoned James, was near the small mining town of Carbon, located between Medicine Bow and Rawlins.

James, Parrott, and the gang broke into a section line tool shed, stole picks and shovels, and proceeded to pry loose one of the rails. After the rail had been partially unfastened and a stout wire wrapped around it to pull it to the side of the railroad bed, one of the gang members spotted a handcar making its way toward them from the west. Not wishing to be detected before the train arrived, the outlaws raced for cover to wait for the handcar to pass.

Pumping the handcar down the track was John Brown, a longtime Union Pacific section foreman. As Brown approached the loosened rail, he recognized the trouble immediately. He knew the westbound No. 3 train would be coming down the track shortly and deduced that men intent on robbing it were hiding nearby. Without revealing that he had spotted the damage to the rail, Brown kept on going. Parrott and James fell for his ploy, and Brown concentrated on making it far down the track and flagging down the train.

After the train was stopped, law enforcement authorities were alerted to the loosened rail and potential robbery. Posses from Laramie and Rawlins soon arrived at the scene of the attempt. No tracks of men or horses could be found, but the posses divided and followed two logical trails. Two of the posse men—Union Pacific detective Henry Vincent and Bob Widdowfield—were convinced that the outlaws had fled in a different direction, one that led south toward Elk Mountain. They soon picked up the tracks of several riders and followed them.

When Vincent and Widdowfield reached Rattlesnake Pass, they entered the defile without pausing. This proved a serious mistake as Parrott and his gang, having spotted the lawmen on the trail behind them, were waiting for them. A shot from Parrott's rifle killed Widdowfield. Vincent turned his horse and tried to escape, but gang member Dutch Charlie Burris shot him as well.

After killing the two posse members, the gang split up. Frank James decided to head for southwestern Wyoming and then eventually out of the state. Burris fled to Montana, where he was located, arrested, and returned to Carbon to stand trial. On being delivered to Carbon, Burris was greeted by an angry mob bent on hanging him. Believing that confessing to killing Widdowfield and taking his chances with a judge might spare him, he did so. Instead of being placed in jail, however, he was taken to a nearby telegraph pole, where he was placed atop a barrel and a noose fitted over his head. Burris was asked if he had anything to say before he was hanged. Just as he was about to speak, the widow of Widdowfield stepped forward and said, "No, the son of a bitch has nothing to say." With that, she kicked the barrel out from beneath Burris.

One year later, Big Nose Parrott was captured in Montana. By this time, the semisuccessful outlaw had achieved a level of notoriety, if not fame. Instead of being returned to Carbon, he was taken to Rawlins in order to protect him from a rumored lynch mob. The strategy did not work out for Parrott, because shortly after he arrived at Rawlins, he was pulled from his cell and also hanged from a telegraph pole.

A Rawlins physician named John E. Osborne had long been fascinated by George "Big Nose" Parrott. Following the hanging, Osborne made a death mask of Parrott's face. This done, Osborne removed the top part of Parrott's skull. In addition, Osborne skinned the outlaw, taking flesh from his chest and legs. Later, Osborne had the skin from the chest fashioned into a small medical bag. The skin from the thighs was used to make a pair of shoes.

In 1950, workers were digging a foundation for a new building in downtown Rawlins when they encountered a tightly sealed whiskey barrel. Inside, they found a number of items, among them a skeleton. The skeleton was later identified as having belonged to George "Big Nose" Parrott.

CHAPTER 43

WILCOX, JUNE 2, 1899

Wilcox, Wyoming, is located sixty miles northwest of Laramie in the southeastern part of the state. So small and insignificant is Wilcox today that it is not even noted on the majority of state maps. In 1899, it was little more than a trackside station and water stop manned by one or two railroad employees. On June 2 of that year, however, it entered the history books as the scene of a noted train robbery, one that some historians are convinced was perpetrated by members of the Wild Bunch, including Butch Cassidy, Will Carver, Ben Kilpatrick, Elzy Lay, Harvey "Kid Curry" Logan, Logan's brother Lonny, and George "Flat Nose" Curry. Harry Longabaugh, the Sundance Kid, may also have been involved, but this has never been verified. The linking of the Wild Bunch to the Wilcox train robbery, in fact, has remained controversial, and accounts differ.

It is generally agreed that the train robbers stopped the westbound Union Pacific Overland Limited No. 1 at 2:09 a.m. near Wilcox by standing on the tracks and swinging a red lantern. Once the train came to a halt, two men (believed to be Cassidy and Logan), both wearing masks, climbed into the cab and pointed their revolvers at the engineer, W. R. Jones, and the fireman, a man named Dietrick. Jones was ordered to proceed across a bridge a short distance away. Standing up to the robbers, Jones refused. At that point, Logan pulled a knife and slashed the engineer across the face. Bleeding from the cut, Jones acquiesced to the demand and started forward. Moments later the entire train crossed the bridge. Once on the other side, Jones was instructed to halt the train again. As he did so, an explosion was heard behind the train. The bridge had been rigged with dynamite, but the explosion failed to collapse it into the ravine below. It is believed that the outlaws were convinced that another train would soon follow the Union Pacific and wanted to make certain it would not be able to catch up to them.

Members of the gang uncoupled the passenger coaches from the express and mail cars and ordered Jones to move the train another two miles up the track, where he was to stop. At that point, four additional outlaws rode up brandishing revolvers and rifles. Remaining on their horses, they stood guard over the train.

Cassidy, Logan, and at least one other robber walked over to the express car and banged on the door, yelling for the messenger to open it. The messenger, Ernest Charles Woodcock, refused and made certain the door was fully bolted shut. Neither having the time nor the willingness to negotiate, the outlaws placed a charge of dynamite at the bottom of the door, lit the fuse, and retreated to safety. The resulting explosion blew the large iron door several yards from the tracks and scattered pieces of the express car for one hundred yards in all directions. One end of the adjacent mail car was also destroyed, as were a number of bridge supports behind the train.

Miraculously, messenger Woodcock, though injured, survived the explosion. He suffered several cuts and a possible concussion. On spotting the semiconscious messenger lying on the floor of the car, at least one of the outlaws wanted to shoot him, but Cassidy interfered, stating that the courageous messenger deserved to live. Besides, he said, he possessed the combination to the safe, which was the target of the robbery.

The bleeding and dazed Woodcock was revived by the outlaws and, when ordered to open the safe, continued to refuse. Wasting no time, the robbers attached a charge of dynamite to the safe and blew away the thick steel door. In the process, they destroyed much of what was left of the express car. When the safe exploded, the money inside was blown into the air and scattered by the wind, forcing the robbers to chase after it, plucking it out of the air and scooping it up from the ground.

After stuffing the bills into their saddlebags, the outlaws signaled their companions, who were standing guard near the locomotive, that it was time to leave. Moments later they were riding away to the north toward Casper. The train robbers got away with over $3,000.

Only one hour before sunrise on June 2, 1899, Union Pacific authorities were notified of the heist. Officials immediately suspected the Wild Bunch was behind the train robbery.

Riding from the scene of the crime, the outlaws split up and headed off in different directions. Posses were formed as soon as word of the robbery spread, but by the time they arrived at the train, the trail had gone cold. Between the robbery and the arrival of the lawmen, a heavy rain had struck the area and washed away any tracks. In time, four hundred men joined the pursuit of the robbers. It was estimated that during their escape, they had traveled over fifteen hundred miles while evading the posses. Union Pacific Railroad detective F. M. Hans was quoted as stating, "Time and again [the robbers] have been surrounded by ten times their number, yet by the display of their desperate nerve and knowledge of woodcraft have managed each time to get away."

According to Hans, the robbers "kept on into the Big Horn Basin, then turned back and retraced their steps through the Powder River country into the Jackson's Hole country, the wildest and most desolate stretch of mountainous country in the West."

The Union Pacific Railroad and Pacific Express companies jointly offered rewards of $2,000 for each of the train robbers, dead or alive. The US government joined in with a $1,000 reward for each outlaw. Though more than $30,000 had been blown out of the safe, railroad authorities insisted that the robbers escaped with very little of the money and that most of it was either destroyed by the explosion or scattered by the winds. None of the outlaws was captured.

CHAPTER 44

TIPTON, AUGUST 29, 1900

Like the Wilcox, Wyoming, train robbery one year earlier, the one at Tipton is beset with controversy. While the evidence is scanty, most believed that this one, like the previous, was conducted by Butch Cassidy and other members of the Wild Bunch. The motive behind the robbery, some believe, lay in the fact that Cassidy had earlier agreed to meet with representatives of the railroad companies during late 1899 or early 1900 at Lost Soldiers Pass in the foothills of Green Mountain. The representatives did not show up.

The meeting had been arranged by Orlando W. Powers, a judge in Salt Lake City. Powers told Cassidy that he would approach railroad officials and try to get them to drop all charges related to train robbery if Cassidy would agree never to rob another train. Powers also suggested that he could arrange for Cassidy to be employed as a railroad guard working for the Union Pacific. Cassidy agreed to the terms and said he would meet with railroad officials at the earliest possible date.

Cassidy arrived at the selected location early and waited for the appearance of the railroad representatives. He waited for most of the day.

Disappointed and angry, Cassidy left a note stating, in part, "Tell the U. P. to go to hell," and departed, now more mistrustful than ever of railroad representatives. Many believe that Cassidy decided to hold up the Union Pacific train near Tipton because the railroad representatives had stood him up. As it turned out, the railroad men were delayed by a storm and arrived the next day.

In 1900 Tipton amounted to little more than a small railroad siding in Wyoming's Sweetwater County, located sixty miles east of Rock Springs and seventy miles west of Rawlins. The town was awarded a post office in June 1886, but it was discontinued in September of the same year for lack of activity. The town's claim to fame is that it was the site of a major train robbery, one likely perpetrated by Butch Cassidy and the notorious Wild Bunch.

Proof is lacking, and evidence is spurious, but most researchers believe the robbers included Cassidy, Ben Kilpatrick, Harvey Logan, Harry Longabaugh, William Cruzan, and possibly a woman, Laura Bullion, at the time Logan's girlfriend. Later, she went on to become the companion of Ben Kilpatrick. The modus operandi was similar to that of other robberies perpetrated by the Wild Bunch.

One of the gang members, believed to be Harvey Logan, rode aboard the train as a passenger. Writer John Burroughs, however, stated that Logan "darted out of the shadows beside the water tank, grasped the handrail at the rear of the tender, and climbed aboard." After tying a bandanna around his face, Logan climbed into the engine compartment and at gunpoint ordered engineer Henry Wallenstine to stop the train at a predetermined location up ahead. A third version has the engineer stopping the train to investigate a mysterious fire alongside the tracks, but this seems unlikely. When the train finally came to a halt, one of the bandits ordered conductor E. K. Kerrigan to uncouple the mail and express cars from the passenger cars.

When Cassidy and his fellow train robbers arrived back at the express car, they were surprised to learn that the messenger was Ernest Charles Woodcock, the same man who had survived the dynamite blast during the Wilcox robbery. Cassidy ordered Woodcock to open the door to the car or it would be blown away again. With his characteristic stubbornness, Woodcock, ever the loyal employee, refused. Cassidy did not wish to see Woodcock injured, so he asked conductor Kerrigan to convince the messenger to open the door. Kerrigan spoke with Woodcock for several minutes, begging him to let the robbers inside. Woodcock responded by saying he would shoot the first man to enter the car.

Cassidy was impressed with Woodcock's bravery and did not want to see him hurt. He asked Kerrigan once again to talk it over with the messenger, and this time Woodcock reluctantly slid open the express car door. Before doing so, however, he hid two large packages of money that the robbers never found.

Cassidy attached an oversize charge of dynamite to the large steel safe found in the car. The subsequent explosion not only blew the door to the safe open but completely demolished the express car as well as the car coupled next to it. After scooping up the money— an estimated $55,000—along with a quantity of jewelry, the gang rode away. This time, as was Cassidy's direction, no one was hurt. The next day, the Union Pacific Railroad issued a press release stating that the robbers got away with only $54, but Woodcock was later quoted as saying the take amounted to $55,000. It was later suggested that the railroad company wanted would-be bandits to believe that the trains were not carrying much money.

Soon after the robbery, the Union Pacific's private army and several posses were once again on the trail of the outlaws. Premier tracker Joe LeFors came close to overtaking the outlaws, but the gang stayed far ahead of him using relays of horses stationed along the way, always managing to outdistance and elude him. At times, the posse came within a few hundred yards of the outlaws but never succeeded in catching up to them.

A few days following the robbery, Union Pacific officials offered a $10,000 reward for each member of the gang that robbed the train at Tipton. An image of Butch Cassidy was placed on the wanted poster. In the wake of the train holdup, more and more posses were in the field searching for Cassidy and other members of the Wild Bunch.

With the increased pursuit and gradual closing in of lawmen over the previous months, Butch Cassidy decided it was time to look for something else to do. Since there now appeared no chance of amnesty or pardon, he considered leaving the United States and settling in some foreign country where he was not known and could make a fresh start. At this point in his life, all he wanted to do was get away and start life anew. He set his sights on South America.

CHAPTER 45

THE END OF BUTCH CASSIDY, TRAIN ROBBER

The American West was alive with lawmen, bounty hunters, and private detectives, all looking for Butch Cassidy and members of the Wild Bunch. In addition, Wells, Fargo and Company, severely impacted by Wild Bunch depredations, sent a team of investigators into the field to run down the outlaws. Pinkerton detectives, at the urging of the banks and railroad companies, remained active in the hunt for the train robbers.

Understanding the magnitude of the efforts of the various agencies and authorities to capture or kill the gang, Butch Cassidy and Harry Longabaugh began discussing the possibility of leaving the country, and South America held an appeal. Argentina and Bolivia were similar to the American West and were opening up to settlement and ranching. After obtaining some information on these countries, followed by some discussion, Cassidy and the Sundance Kid decided that South America was their destination.

After resting up for several weeks in Wyoming, the pair traveled to Colorado, where they purchased train tickets to Fort Worth, Texas, arriving in November 1900. There, along with Will Carver, Ben Kilpatrick, and Harvey "Kid Curry" Logan, they hung out at Hell's Half Acre, a notorious section of town active with cowhands, buffalo hunters, gamblers, salesmen, and prostitutes.

By December, the members of the Wild Bunch had scattered, with Cassidy and Longabaugh traveling to San Antonio, where they

205

frequented a bordello owned by Fanny Porter. From there they went to New Orleans, Louisiana, and then to Phoenixville, Pennsylvania, Longabaugh's boyhood home, where he visited his brother Harvey and his sisters Emma and Samanna. From Phoenixville, they made their way to Buffalo and then on to New York City, joined at some point by Etta Place. There they purchased steamer tickets to Buenos Aires, Argentina. During the subsequent months, the three traveled throughout Argentina and Bolivia in search of suitable ranch land and a place to settle. They found what they were looking for in the Cholila Valley, Chubut Province, Argentina, where they raised cattle, sheep, and horses. It was 1902. A short time later, Etta Place returned to the United States.

As Cassidy and Longabaugh pursued their living as ranchers in the Cholila Valley, they learned that the Pinkertons had sent at least one detective to South America in search of them. Through their sources, the two outlaws were informed that the Pinkertons were closing in. In late 1904, Cassidy and Longabaugh believed they were no longer safe from pursuit at their present location. They sold their livestock, buildings, and a number of personal possessions and fled. By 1905, they had crossed the Andes and settled for a time in Chile. They continued to travel back and forth between Chile and Argentina, and several banks were robbed in these countries during this time. When shown photographs of Cassidy and Longabaugh, the victims identified them as the robbers.

By 1906 Cassidy and Longabaugh had landed jobs at the Concordia Tin Mines near the town of Tres Cruces in the foothills of the Bolivian Andes. Cassidy was hired to transport payroll remittances, and Longabaugh was assigned to break and train mules. The two men were employed at the tin mines from 1906 to 1908. The longer they worked there, however, the more people became aware of who they really were. In October 1907, Cassidy and Longabaugh entered a police station in Santa Cruz, Bolivia, and were surprised to find their images on wanted posters tacked up on the wall. They decided to move on.

It is believed that the two friends robbed a Bolivian railway train near La Paz in August 1908, escaping with $90,000. With this successful robbery under their belts, they turned their attention to the possibility of robbing some mine payrolls. According to some researchers, they did exactly that on at least two occasions. The movements and activities of Cassidy and Longabaugh by late 1908 have proven difficult to document. A number of writers think that the two outlaws set their sights on the payroll of the Aramayo mines, located near the southern Bolivian town of Tupiza.

During this time a number of other American outlaws had sought refuge in South America. On arriving, they lost no time in reverting to what they did best: robbing trains and banks. A number of these crimes, as it turned out, were attributed to Cassidy and Longabaugh, although the perpetrators may well have been Harvey "Kid Curry" Logan, Robert Evans, and William Wilson.

The story of what most believe happened to Cassidy and Longabaugh evolved in the following manner. Two men thought to be them robbed the Aramayo payroll on November 4, 1908. In addition to the $7,000 in money, the pair of robbers escaped with one of the company's mules. The mule was branded with the number 4, the company's official brand. Shortly after the robbery, two North Americans arrived at the town of Tupiza. Soon after unpacking their gear, they discovered that the residents suspected them of being the payroll robbers. Hurriedly, they repacked and fled. Three days later, on November 7, two strangers arrived at the small Indian village of San Vicente. The newcomers settled into a room at the police station, which also served as an inn.

While the two men were dining on tinned sardines and beer, a local constable happened to pass by and noticed the "4" brand on one of mules belonging to the strangers. He knew it was the brand of the Aramayo mines and suspected that the two newcomers may have had something to do with the robbery. What many believed happened next, as portrayed in the popular film *Butch Cassidy and the Sundance Kid* starring Paul Newman and Robert Redford, is a fiction based on the florid 1930s novel by Arthur Chapman.

Based on evidence, this is what happened. A police inspector, a San Vicente citizen, and two Bolivian soldiers arrived at the room of the two strangers to question them about the mule. One of the soldiers approached the open doorway only to be fired upon by one of the occupants. The soldier died several minutes later. The San Vicente citizen chose to return to his home, and the two men remaining elected to stand guard over the room until reinforcements could arrive.

The following morning, the guards entered the room and found the inhabitants dead. It looked as though one of the men had shot the other and then committed suicide. Inside the room was found the Aramayo payroll money. Later that day, the two bodies were carried to the San Vicente Indian cemetery and buried in an unmarked grave. Neither of the two dead men was ever identified.

Recent investigations into evidence related to what happened to Butch Cassidy and the Sundance Kid yield the conclusion that they were not killed at San Vicente and instead traveled throughout South America and eventually returned to the United States. Here is a truth: there exists no evidence whatsoever that Butch Cassidy and the Sundance Kid were killed in Bolivia and buried in the San Vicente cemetery. On the other hand, powerful and compelling evidence exists that the two men not only returned to the United States but also lived out the remainder of their lives under aliases, mingling with relatives and former Hole-in-the-Wall Gang members. Details of the life of Butch Cassidy after he returned to his homeland, the name he lived under, and his activities, as well as a detailed examination of the evidence related to the truth of the San Vicente incident, can be found in my 2014 book *Butch Cassidy: Beyond the Grave*.

GLOSSARY OF RAILROAD TERMS

BLIND

A walkway between two passenger cars. The space was generally open but sometimes covered with accordion-pleated leather or heavy canvas. A ladder ran from the blind to the top of the car. Hobos would occasionally jump onto the blinds just before a train departed the station and hitch a ride to some destination. This practice was called "riding the blinds."

BOILER

A closed vessel found on steam engines in which water was heated. A boiler was sometimes referred to as a steam generator.

CONDUCTOR

A railroad employee in charge of the train and its crew. On passenger trains, the conductor was also responsible for such tasks as assisting passengers and collecting tickets.

COWCATCHER

Also called a "pilot," a device made of strong metal and mounted onto the front of the locomotive for the purpose of deflecting obstacles that could potentially derail the train. The cowcatcher was designed such that it pushed any obstacle upward and sideways and ultimately out of the way.

ENGINEER

A railroad employee responsible for operating the locomotive.

EXPRESS CAR

The train vehicle designated for transporting money, certificates, and other valuables. This car was leased or owned by the express company.

EXPRESS COMPANY

A business for transporting goods and cash. Express companies often leased or owned railroad cars for the purpose of carrying such items.

EXPRESS MESSENGER

A railroad employee who accompanied the express car, each of which generally carried at least one messenger and sometimes as many as three. The term "messenger," as employed by the railroads, meant "courier." It was the job of the messenger to maintain the paperwork associated with what was being transported. Messengers were responsible for everything in the express car, which is why they often refused to open the doors during robbery attempts. If an express car was robbed, the messenger often lost his job as a result.

EXPRESS SAFE

A safe carrying money, bullion, and/or other valuables that could only be unlocked by officials at certain stations along the railroad route. The express messengers riding in the car were unable to unlock the express safes.

FIREMAN

The member of the train crew who shoveled coal into the furnace and tended the boiler on steam locomotives. His job was to make certain the train had the power necessary to negotiate hills and turns.

FLAGMAN

An employee of the railroad assigned to protect contractors or anyone working on a railroad right-of-way. When a train approached a location where workers might be fixing a track, the train crew summoned the flagman for permission to pass the work area.

LOCAL SAFE

A safe carrying valuables and being transported in the express car. The express messenger generally carried the key to open this safe and was responsible for the express car and its contents.

MAIL CAR

Similar to, but separate from, the express car. Mail cars transported the US mail.

PINKERTON DETECTIVES

Employees of the Pinkerton National Detective Agency, founded in 1885 by Alan Pinkerton, which worked closely with midwestern railroads. The duties of the Pinkertons included investigating theft of property and dealing with labor problems and customer complaints. Because Pinkerton agents were not affiliated with the federal government, they were not subject to federal rules and regulations. The agency was often criticized for its unorthodox methods related to pursuing and capturing train robbers, but in the end the railroad companies were satisfied with their efforts.

RAILROAD POLICE

Railroad companies' own police and security forces, modeled on the Pinkertons. While providing a modicum of security for the mail and express cars, as well as for the passengers, the railroad police were more often involved with the pursuit and capture of train robbers. Railroad police, also called railroad detectives, generally carried handguns and clubs and sported a badge issued by the railroad company. Their methods were often bullying and brutal, and the railroad police, though called on to help pursue train robbers, were generally looked down upon by legitimate law enforcement officers.

TENDER

Sometimes referred to as the coal tender, a specialized rail car immediately behind the steam locomotive used to carry coal, a water supply, and tools.

TRESTLE

A style of bridge over a gully, river, or any other type of gorge for roads and railroads. It consists mainly of a braced framework of wood or metal.

BIBLIOGRAPHY

Books

Beebe, Lucius, and Charles Clegg. *U.S. West: The Saga of Wells, Fargo*. New York: E. P. Dutton and Company, 1948.

Block, Eugene B. *Great Train Robberies of the West*. New York: Coward-McCann, Inc., 1959.

Burroughs, John Rolfe. *Where the Old West Stayed Young*. New York: Morrow, 1962.

Chaput, Donald. *Spawn Gone Wrong: The Odyssey of Burt Alvord, Lawman, Train Robber, Fugitive*. Claremont, CA: Westernlore Press Company, 2000.

DeArment, Robert K. *Deadly Dozen: Twelve Forgotten Gunfighters of the Old West*. Vol. 1. Norman: University of Oklahoma Press, 2003.

DeNevi, Don. *Western Train Robberies*. Millbrae, CA: Celestial Arts, 1976.

Drago, Harry Sinclair. *Outlaws on Horseback*. New York: Dodd, Mead and Company, 1964.

Ernst, Donna B. *Sundance, My Uncle*. College Station, TX: Early West, 1992.

———. *The Sundance Kid: The Life of Harry Longabaugh*. Norman: University of Oklahoma Press, 2009.

Hume, James B., and John N. Thacker. *Wells, Fargo & Co: Stagecoach and Train Robberies, 1870–1884*. Jefferson, NC: McFarland and Company, Publishers, 2010.

Jameson, W. C. *Butch Cassidy: Beyond the Grave*. Boulder, CO: Taylor Trade Publishing, 2014.

———. *New Mexico Treasure Tales*. Caldwell, ID: Caxton Press, 2003.

Jenson, Kenneth. *Colorado Gunsmoke*. Boulder, CO: Pruett Publishing Company, 1986.

Kelly, Charles. *The Outlaw Trail: A History of Butch Cassidy and the Wild Bunch*. Lincoln: University of Nebraska Press, 1938.

Kirby, Edward M. *The Rise and Fall of the Sundance Kid*. Iola, WI: Western Publications, 1983.

———. *The Saga of Butch Cassidy and the Wild Bunch*. Palmer Lake, CO: Filter Press, 1977.

Nash, Robert. *Encyclopedia of Western Lawmen and Outlaws*. Boston: De Capo Press, 1994.

Patterson, Richard. *Butch Cassidy: A Biography*. Lincoln: University of Nebraska Press, 1998.

———. *Historical Atlas of the Outlaw West*. Boulder, CO: Johnson Books, 1985.

———. *The Train Robbery Era*. Boulder, CO: Pruett Publishing Company, 1991.

———. *Wyoming's Outlaw Days*. Boulder, CO: Johnson Books, 1982.

Wilson, R. Michael. *Great Train Robberies of the Old West*. Helena, MT: TwoDot, 2007.

Articles

Ball, Larry D. "Audacious and Best Executed: Tom Horn and Colorado's Cotopaxi Train Robbery," *Colorado Heritage Magazine* 20, no. 4 (2000).

Breihan, Carl. "The Outlaw Who Became a Pair of Shoes," *True West* (January 1983).

Burton, Jeff. "Bureaucracy, Blood Money, and Black Jack's Gang," *English Westerners' Society Brand Book* (winter/summer 1983–1984).

Caldwell, George A. "New Mexico's First Train Robbery," *NOLA Quarterly* (winter 1989).

Earl, Phillip I. "The Montello Robbery," *Northeastern Nevada Historical Society Quarterly* (summer 1972).

Fitzgerald, Gerald. "CPRR Number One Had a Bad Day," *Northeastern Nevada Historical Society Quarterly* (spring 1975).

Gibson, Elizabeth. "Kid Curry: The Wildest of the Bunch," *Western Outlaw-Lawmen History Association Journal* (spring 1999).

Kildare, Maurice. "Arizona's Great Train Robbery," *True West* (September 1968).

Milles, Victor W. "The McCoy Gang," *Old West* (summer 1970).

Walker, Dale L. "Buckey O'Neill and the Holdup at Diablo Canyon," *Real West* (November 1978).

Newspapers

Bellfonte Republican (Pennsylvania). "Daring Band of Cowboys." November 28, 1883.

New York Times. "Great Train Robberies of the West." June 18, 1904.

———. "Great Train Robberies of the West." July 27, 1904.

———. "Train Robbers Sentenced; Two Youths Get 50–75 Years for Death in Holdup." February 21, 1928.

———. October 25, 1902.

———. September 23, 1900.

———. August 8, 1892.

Pittsburg Press. "Youths Held in Slaying; Find Story Books Were Wrong." December 13, 1937.

Sacramento Daily Union. "Arizona Bandits: Bold Night Attack on Westbound Train." April 29, 1887.

San Francisco Chronicle. July 31, 1904.

———. August 1, 2, 4, 1904.

Sarasota Herald. "Train Bandits Held for Trial; Bail Denied." December 21, 1937.

The Tombstone News. Traywick, Ben T. "The Willcox Train Robbery." May 27, 2017.

Weekly Elko Independent (Elko, Nevada). January 28, 1883.

———. February 4, 1883.

———. March 4, 1883.

INDEX

ACKNOWLEDGMENTS

Any book project worth its salt is a product of the efforts and contributions of several people, a team all committed to issuing the best book possible. I'm proud and, frankly, relieved to be a member of this team. I get to do the fun part—the writing. All of the others perform their roles with dignity, apply their expertise, and do all of the hard work I get to avoid. Much of what they do is a mystery to me, and I want to keep it that way. I am grateful to all of them and delighted to be in their company.

I always endeavor to send the cleanest manuscripts possible to my publishing house editors. Laurie Jameson has edited for *New York Times* best-selling authors, and before a manuscript ever leaves my studio, she has applied her magic to it. I am often complimented and thanked for the condition and relative cleanliness of my submissions, and this is due to Laurie.

It has been a pleasure working with Erin Turner, who has shepherded my creations through the inner workings of a variety of Rowman & Littlefield Publishing Group imprints (Globe Pequot, TwoDot, Lone Star Books, and more). She has manifested an impressive patience with my often fumbling manner as I continue to try to figure out how my computer is supposed to do stuff.

Intrepid agent Sandra Bond continues to amaze and delight with regular news of book contracts she has secured for me. She manages to keep me busy throughout the year, knows her way around contracts, deals with television and other film-production people for me, and maintains a keen sense of humor throughout.

Thanks to all of you. I can't imagine doing any of this without you. Besides, you make it fun.

ABOUT THE AUTHOR

W. C. Jameson is the award-winning author of over one hundred books, fifteen hundred articles, three books of poetry, and four hundred songs. He has served as a consultant for film and television and appears regularly on a number of cable channels as an analyst and talking head. He has contributed music to the soundtracks of seven films, has recorded eight albums of original songs, and has been the subject of two documentaries. When not locked away in his writing studio working on books, he travels the country performing his songs at music festivals, colleges and universities, concert halls, and roadhouses and on television. He lives in Llano, Texas.